RURAL TRANSFORMATION AND PEOPLES ENTITLEMENTS

By the same author

Capacity Building for Local Leaders
Dynamics of New Panchayati Raj System (Two Vols.)
New Panchayati Raj in Tamil Nadu (With Act in Original)

About the Author

Prof. Ganapathi Palanithurai, Dean, Faculty of Social Sciences, Coordinator in Rajiv Gandhi Chair, Gandhigram Rural Institute is an academic activist working with the people in rural areas for building the capacity of the leaders and people to reinvent sustainable grassroots democracy and to achieve sustainable rural development. He is heading the Department of Political Science and Development Administration, in Gandhigram Rural University, Tamil Nadu. His policy advocacy role at the governmental level is increasingly felt at present in all the three levels, namely sub-regional, regional and national as he does more field work than theorisation. He has been associating himself with Centre Planning Commission, State Planning Commission of Tamil Nadu, Population Foundation of India, Ford Foundation. UNICEF, Rajiv Gandhi Foundation, CAPART, Ministry of Rural Areas and Employment and DANIDA (Danish-Indo Development Agency) in specific areas of activities in connection with empowerment of people. He is in the network of the Non-Governmental Organisations for Panchayat activities. He involves himself in capacity building exercise for local body leaders. He has evolved training module and manual for local body leaders. He has thirty-two books, seventy-nine articles in reputed journals, twelve working papers, seven monographs, seven review articles of three major areas, namely Legislative Behaviour, Ethnicity and Panchayati Raj System to his credit. He was a recipient of Fellowship from Sastri Indo-Canadian Institute, New Delhi and World Academy of Art and Science, USA. He is the Chairman of the Tamil Nadu Council for Sustainable Livelihoods. He has visited the US and Canada, on academic assignments. He was a visiting fellow in the MiGill University, Canada in 1989. He is a life member of Indian Institute of Public Administration, Indian Association of Public Administration, Indian Association of Political Science, Indian Association of American Studies and Indian Association of Canadian Studies. He is a member of the expert committee constituted by the Government of Tamil Nadu, to monitor the training programme for local body leaders. He is the Chairperson of the Hunger Project Council in Tamil Nadu.

RURAL TRANSFORMATION AND PEOPLES ENTITLEMENTS

G. PALANITHURAI
Professor and Head
Department of Political Science and
Development Administation.
Gandhigram Rural University,
Tamil Nadu

CONCEPT PUBLISHING COMPANY, NEW DELHI-110059

ISBN-81-8069-058-X

First Published 2004

Published and Printed by
Ashok Kumar Mittal
Concept Publishing Company
A/15-16, Commercial Block, Mohan Garden
NEW DELHI-110059 (INDIA)

Phones : 25351460, 25351794
Fax : 091-11-25357103
E-mail : publishing@conceptpub.com

TO

THE DIVINE MOTHER

PREFACE

I was born seven years after India attained Independence. I became conscious of my surroundings roughly from the age of four. For about thirty-eight years, I have been observing the changes in the society consciously without much curiosity and objective. More particularly I have witnessed momentous changes in the rural areas as I have been in the rural society for about thirty years. Ever since I went to college for higher education, I have realised the differences between the urban areas and the rural society in terms of the changes both societies have witnessed in the course of history. On most occasions I was puzzled by some phenomena whenever I witnessed both in the urban and rural societies. From physical living conditions to higher mental perceptions of the leaders, society has moved over from one level to another both vertically and horizontally. The changes are phenomenal. While analyzing the changes historically in time series one would notice the increasing speed of change. The change was a natural process initiated by the human beings to increase the comfort of their living. But the speed of change was accelerated through the instruments which have been devised by men in the form of government in the course of their experiment with life.

Communication is one of the instruments which have totally altered the vision and perception of the people about the human life and actions in the society. Communication network has established linkages among the societies and communities for exchange of ideas and thus the gap between the societies and communities in terms of flow of information has been bridged. Today, societies have no barriers and obstacles in getting information from any place at any distance. Ideas, perceptions, views, values and attitudes are being spread fast and they have created a change in the thought process and performance of the people everywhere. The moot question here is, which idea has influenced man and society? Ideas have an action frame. Yet, actions have not always been unanimous like ideas. So conflicting ideas and actions will be there in any society. But, ultimately, dominant ideas and actions would attract humanity and the same would continue till these ideas and actions meet failure. Yet each society, whether it is western or eastern, has its own deviation from the main path and process of development.

In recent years literature has proliferated on development, its dimensions and causative factors. In the course of analysis, scholars began to use some of the terms akin to development which are relevant for any social analysis at present. They are modernization, westernization and industrialization. The three concepts emerged as ways of life for humanity for about three centuries. There were arguments in favour of and against these paths of development. Yet these paths and concepts have gained momentum as societies prefer to adopt them for their betterment.

In the process of modernization, industrialization and westernization, societies have witnessed catalysmic change both externally and internally. It is not uniform in all collectivities and groups in terms of the speed of change. Likewise all aspects of life have not been changed. Changes vary from individual to individual, group to group and society to society. Changes in the life situation of the people are explicit in nature. But the changes in attitude, perception, belief of the people cannot be gauged unless they are observed in their actions very keenly. On certain aspects of human life change is noticed with high speed and on yet other aspects speed is minimal. Steps have always been taken to increase the speed of change deliberately with the intervention of the State. In the past few decades speed of change has increased unexpectedly. But, on a few aspects the societies have not moved not even an inch. The basic question is to what extent the people perceive that they have to transform themselves in different aspects of life and on what aspects and how the changes were allowed to happen in the society within the boundaries of their culture?

Thirty-five years ago I attended a marriage along with my father and mother where I saw that seventy-five per cent of the invitees were half naked as they had the practice of wearing *dothi* and towel and not shirt and banian. Only a few were dressed in shirts. In those days brides and bridegrooms were brought to the place of the ceremony (mostly temples and sometimes the bridegroom's house) in a bullock cart. A cycle was a luxury. Motorbikes were unheard of. To see a bus we travelled for about ten kilometres on foot during those days. Water was taken from a community tank which was maintained by the community through an association. Bullock cart was the only mode of transport available at that time. Medical facilities in the modern sense were far away from the people. Country medicine practised in every family was the only medical facility for the common people. Education was considered a privileged facility for the rich alone and they could alone afford to meet the expenditure. Mobility of the people was restricted due to paucity of communication facilities. Most of the needs of the people were met by the activities of the community. Government was not recognized as the provider of all and protector. More or less villages were on the road to reaching the state of a republic.

But now the conditions are different. Every village is linked with a town by a link road. Everyman is provided with communication facilities to move from the rural areas to urban centres. Dress, education, medical facilities, government offices, market places, cosmetics and entertainment, are the prime attraction of the towns and cities which draw people from the rural areas. Children from the rural areas are admitted in English medium schools in the towns irrespective of the level of their parensts' income. Wearing wrist watch and using footwear and modern dress are the ordinary affair at present. New types of markets have emerged in the towns. Towns are congested due to heavy inflow of men and women from the rural areas for various purposes. Stainless steel once a product meant for the rich has now moved within the grasp of the poor. In every house whether it is rich or poor, one will find stainless steel vessels. Likewise, radio, tape recorder and television are now-a-days common men's properties. Even a mason or a carpenter or a milk vendor goes to the work spot on a moped. A poor woman from her savings purchase ornaments of gold covering at a cheap rate. Totally a revolution has taken place in the rural areas, raising expectation among the mass about the articles that they should possess.

In the fifty years of democratic governance, facilities have been proliferated. Government Departments have been increased, their size and number to meet the rising expectations of the people.

Facilities provided by the government have narrowed down the gap between the communities, groups and societies. This has brought several changes in the externalities of the man and the society. As a result competitions between and among individuals and groups have increased not only in productive skills but also in sharing the benefits of the government.

The external changes which we have been witnessing will not be helpful to the community to achieve sustainable development. The facilities provided by the government have not been fully utilised to bring development. People do not have the needed requisite knowledge to maintain the facilities provided by the government and to make use of all the facilities to achieve economic growth and social development. Poverty, unemployment, underemployment and violent social conflict still persist in the rural areas. The key question here is, why this syndrome? To give answer to this question, an attempt has been made to study the life pattern of the people in two villages in depth over a period of fifty years. The two villages in Dindigul district, namely Nariyuthu and Chitharevu have been chosen for this work as both villages have complex socio-economic and cultural characteristics. Data have been collected from the groups as well as individuals. For most of the aspects the investigating team heavily relied on the memory of the elders who have crossed sixty in their age. It is to be mentioned here that this study does not proceed in the backdrop of any theory.

There is yet another aspect, namely the entitlement which has also formed part of this study as the government became a sole authority in deciding the destiny of the people through its decisions, policies and money allocations. People have developed a dependency syndrome and they expect everything from the government. Moreover, the state has been empowered to look after most of the affairs of the people and to provide certain facilities and services and now these servcies are becoming entitlements of the people. Thus people have entitlements and how far these entitlements have been met by the state authorities is a major question. Because the state has declared that the governments are not able to meet the demands of the people and it intended to create more local institutions to ensure the basic entitlements of the people.

Against this background a study has been undertaken to analyse how far the state authorities have committed to ensure the entitlements of the rural people. To carry out this study four villages (Mallanampatti, Ariyanallur, Pachamalayankottai and Avayampatti from three different Block Panchayats in Dindigul district) have been selected, interview schedules have been prepared and administered with the people from different segments of the villages selected for this study. Their reactions are classified and explained in the third chapter of this work under the caption "People's Entitlement".

After presenting the aspects of transformation from the perspective of the people, as a researcher I have made some observation about the change which I have witnessed in the society. I have presented my observations in a separate chapter under the caption "Researcher's Observation". Further when the society is marching towards the next century what will be future of the rural society has been predicted. In this chapter, contextually a very important aspect has been analysed. Grassroots democracy has been established through legislations and by which powers have been decentralised. But at the same time rural areas cannot be separated from the impact of the globalization process. It is a two-way process. Globalization and decentralization are the two sides of the same coin. Both are not mutually exclusive. Hence, this is more important from the perspective of economy and polity. Western experience portrays that the development of the human collectivities by improving the human resources, economy of the society could be developed. The above mentioned aspects have been visualised from the view point of the rural mass. This chapter is drawn from the paper presented in a world summit organised by the World Academy of Art and Science in Vancouver Canada from 4th to 7th November, 1998.

To present all these ideas in the form of a book many individuals have helped me. Of them the villagers of Nariyuthu, Chitheravu, Mallanampatti, Ariyanallur, Pachamalayankottai and Avayampatti have contributed immensely not only by providing data but also spending their valuable time with the research team. On even for minute questions they tried their level best to provide accurate answer. Especially, the women folk deserves appreciation as they gave answer to the questions on matters relating to sensitive issues.

The respondents took it seriously and provided adequate information. They deserve our sincere thanks.

Next to the respondents, my research team M. Gurusamy, S. Devaraj, M.A. Thirunavukkarasu and A. Thangathurai, who have rich experience in working with the people apart from being individuals hailing from rural areas, have worked with me tirelessly not only in collecting material from the field but also explaining even the minute details regarding the activities of the people in the selected villages. Their devotion and dedication brought wealth of information to me. I profusely thank them for their service in collecting and tabulating the data. Apart from the research team there are two units which deserve my mention here. One is my faculty and another one is my family. My faculty members have given full cooperation, in the form of doing their job perfectly, and allowing me to complete this work. They also shared their views with me on several of the issues discussed in this work. Dr. M.A. Jeyaraj, Dean Faculty of English and Foreign Languages has gone through the manuscript and offered his comments and for which I express my deep sense of gratitude to him. My wife, Mrs. Mala a devoted family lady, spared me to do my academic work without any disturbance. She has been taking pain to look after my kids. She deserves my appreciation. Likewise my kids who have been consistently doing good in their studies and they have never disturbed me while I was at work. I profusely thank my lovely kids Senthil Vadivu and Aurobindh. My secretarial staff have always been with me to support in all my academic endeavours and for which I express my thanks to them. Mr. P. Rajan, my steno, has taken pain to feed the matter in computer and correct the manuscript many times as per my instruction with a sense of devotion and for which I express my thanks to him. Last but not the least my graduate students who have contributed immensely to this study as most of them are from the rural areas. I have gained much whenever I interacted with them on those issues akin to transformation of the rural society. Hence I place on record my deep sense of appreciation to my students.

Gandhigram **G. PALANITHURAI**

CONTENTS

1

INTRODUCTION

India seems to be generally in the throes of crises and sometimes, it is in acute instability. The governance is under stress. Instability in governance, corruption in politics and administration, moral degradation in public life, and, violent social behaviour have projected India as a land of lawlessness, chaos and confusion. It is in the lowest ebb of the development path and process even though we declare that India will soon achieve growth on par with other countries. India has celebrated the golden jubilee of its Independence and, at this juncture, we would do well to review the achievements and lapses in the efforts of the state and the society in administering development. One can see many facets of India—rich India, poor India, divided India, democratic India, mafia India, conflict-prone India and so on. One can be proud of India for the simple reason that still India exists as a nation and as a sovereign democratic republic in the past fifty years after winning Independence. This very existence is a great success. For many academics in the West, Indian polity, society and economy are paradoxes. A deep acumen is needed to understand India. The Indian experience in administering development is almost an experience of State initiation and people's follow-up. In the course of fifty years Indian society has witnessed far-reaching changes in polity, economy, society and culture in many dimensions from perception to behaviour and performance of the people as a result of continuous and intensive State activities *vis-a-vis* the society. The State activities through the Government are based on a very strong conviction that people are always at the receiving end because of their poor understanding of the development process and so the State has to perform many roles. The State has chosen an appropriate institution to administer development. Representative democracy is the institution selected for governance in Indian society. Democratic institutions borrowed from Western countries will have to socialize the people politically in the course of years with the help of the political elite. This was the belief of the political pandits of India.

The objective conditions of the society in India during the freedom struggle engendered two approaches to transform the Indian society from awful conditions to better living conditions on a sustainable basis or from sub-human to human living conditions. The first approach was that of people-oriented activities in consonance with principles of nature where the State can guide and help humanity. In this approach community organisation should have common norms and regulations and community actions should always be in tune with nature. The core principle emphasizes the role of the people in all the activities of the society despite weaknesses or shortcomings. People should be projected first and all activities are to be carried out by the people through their organisation. The State is only a coordinating and a facilitating agency. Primarily, the needs of the people have to be assessed and prioritised by the people themselves. Their assessment and activities are based on their perception of development. Their activities are to be governed by a set of values. All the actions of the people and the State are to be regulated through a harmonious relationship between nature and the people.

The second approach emphasizes the role of the State in ameliorating the conditions of the society in the context of the emergence of the modern Nation-State or State system. The stress is on developing a society from sub-human conditions to human conditions by integrating the collectivities into a nation and initiating action through the State through programmes and schemes. The core proposition is that the needed human resources for development to foster growth and development without the strong intervention of the State are lacking in India. This approach emphasizes the role of the State in growth and development. The Nation-State will have to work within the framework of modernization, industrialization and westernization. Human actions are governed by the relationship between the State and the market from the first development decade. Western development models drew the attention of our political pandits and they moved into the track of Western models. Responsibilities were shifted from the people to the State in order to accelerate economic growth. Thus it was a process of empowerment of the State. But the Western countries quickly switched over from big government to small government approach after seeing the negative implications of the big Government.

In the formative years of nation building in India, it was believed that massive social transformation activities could be generated in the rural areas through the first approach and by which human resources could be developed to achieve growth and development. For the economic development of the country, a massive planning exercise was considered essential, wherein planned programmes could be carried out by the effective intervention of the State. Thus the concept of mixed economy gained currency.

The rural urban dichotomy and the implications of the planning exercises for growth have intensified the growth of the State system. Gradual expansion of the State system has slowly arrested community action. The ruling elite who harbour a commitment to achieving prosperity through industrialization have brought the State to the forefront leaving the people uninvited to the development process of the society. People have vision, technology, science, medicine, culture and commitment to common collective living. But, since people's technology, science, medicine, and management of the community have not been systematised they have not been considered as factors for development. In the perception of the elite, laboratory oriented science, industry oriented technology, and institution oriented literacy are considered essential for development. The profound vision that the illiterate mass had at the dawn of Independence has not been focused and considered. The historic monuments and cultural symbols which were developed over the years by the communities are solid examples of the contribution of the human vision and the capacity of the people even in the monarchical days. But the people of India, in the formative years after Independence, were not considered as participants in the development process. Thus the State acquired enormous respect and importance and it was developed as an omnipotent force to provide everything to the people. In the fourth decade after Independence, the Indian political system became a total State system leaving the people as individuals not as communities. But the State system, by its allocative and administrative activities, has created many changes covertly and overtly in the individuals and collectivities. Developed mass media have started disseminating information from one end to another and from one section to another. Individuals have formed groups based on certain symbols as identities to demand the major share from the allocation of values of the State leaving every responsibility to the State.

The widespread violent social conflict in the Indian social system for social justice has awakened the intellectuals and administrators to review the activities of the State in administering development. It is inferred that governments cannot be complacent with the achievement they have made in polity, economy and society in India over the years through their policies and programmes. In the fifty years of democratic governance and planned economic activities the State has not provided even the basic minimum facilities to all the people of India from South to North and from East to West. In social development India is in the 138th place which is considered as a very serious lapse on the part of the government. Still people are living in sub-human conditions both in rural and urban areas. Whatever developments we have seen in physical infrastructure are helpful only to the rich and not to the poor. Even to make use of the provided infrastructure, people should have adequate economic resources. Hence the rich and the privileged have cornered all those facilities.

The rural urban divide, and the gap between the poor and the rich have escalated the social tension and conflicts into violent proportions, diverting the focus of the government from development administration to crises management. Gradually people have, instead of participating in the development process, been organising themselves as groups to exert pressure on the government to get what they want. Only the elite have participated in the development process. A mind-set has been created by the political elite that it is the duty of the people to mobilise and organise themselves to share the outcome of the activities of the State. Thereby the mass have been mobilised continuously by the political organisations to achieve development. The repeated and continuous demand for social justice and equalization generated from the organised social groups all over India signifies the failure of the State in administering development as well as in rendering social justice. But, the advantage that the people in India have is that democracy provides enough scope and opportunity to express their feelings and grievances without any fear in any form. That is why the 73rd Constitutional Amendment was enacted to emphasise the new role of the community at the micro level to achieve economic development and administer social justice. Yet one cannot underestimate the contribution of the State to polity, economy and society over the years. While going through the statistics compiled by the government and other agencies on vital aspects of economy, polity and society, one can notice the phenomenal transformation in the society in the three sectors mentioned above. The achievements are at the macro level and not at the micro level. Macro realities do not corroborate micro realities. Micro realities are shaking the very foundation of the nation. The transformation witnessed in polity, society and economy have not brought solutions to the existing crises in the rural societies and, in turn, they have intensified the crises. The gap between the rich and the poor, the rural and the urban has increased. However, the achievements are noteworthy. In the process of identifying the solutions to the existing problems and to achieve economic development and social justice, empowerment of people has been suggested in the context of a major policy shift throughout the world. This empowerment of people had been suggested in the formative years of Independence itself by indicating the effectiveness and implications of community based activities for development. What the Western development models have pronounced at present was emphasised long back in India after it attained Independence. In the course of fifty years, people's attitude and perception towards life style, behaviour and performance have changed thoroughly which call for a total reversal to match the new expectations based on the policy shift.

This new dispensation has to change the direction of the society and polity in the development process of the Indian nation. Decentralization of power or small government approach or empowerment approach or empowerment of people has to rejuvenate the economy and render social justice at all levels. It could be done only if the people move into the new track by understanding the new system. People, who have all along acted as consumers should become producers and consumers. This new arrangement of governance provides enormous powers and opportunities to the people to take up responsibilities to achieve economic development through employment generation. By identifying the local resources and skills, employment opportunities have to be created. This process envisages a variety of actions to be initiated. It is not cultural revivalism but the revival of traditional science, technology, skill and networking of human actions for achieving economic growth. This process required a major shift in development initiative. How to make the people move from the track in which they have been travelling to the newly identified track of development? To make the people move from the established track to the new one, a battery of steps have to be taken. First, the perception and the attitude of the people have to be changed. Second, the behaviour and the performance of the people have to be changed. Thirdly, institutions and organisations, both traditional and modern, have to be modified to suit the present requirement. Before identifying the aspects to be changed, one should look into the process by which the people conducted themselves to bring about development during the past fifty years. Attitude, perception, behaviour and performance of the individuals and groups have been under constant transformation. So also institutions and organisations have been modified. Transformation does not take place at the same speed in all aspects of human society in all periods. It varies from one aspect to another and, in the same way, from one period to another.

It is all the more important to identify the aspects in which changes are fast and wherein they are slow. It is also necessary to identify the aspects of human life conducive to the new requirements? The need is not for numerical data but the dimensions of the thought process of the people. Reversals and modifications can be done in instruments easily, but it is very difficult to do it in human mind. The blockade in the thought process of the society has to be cleared. To identify the thought process all aspects of human life in the settlement have to be studied carefully.

Studies have been conducted in Anthropology and Sociology and volumes of literature have been produced. The author of this write-up is a student of neither Sociology nor Cultural Anthropology. He is a student of Political Science looking for appropriate institutions of good governance as an alternative to the existing institutions of governance. As such there are two types of studies conducted on rural change or transformation, viewing the transformation from two main perspectives, namely visualising the obvious transformations totally and collectively against the backdrop of the entire social system and analysing the micro units very deeply. The present work follows neither the macro analysis nor the micro analysis. This work focuses on all aspects of the micro units (villages). But, at the same time, the analysis of the factors in this study is brought under the major premises developed in Sociology, Cultural Anthropology and Political Science. This work is in no way a challenge to the existing theoretical premises. This work is intended to find out the ways and means to identify the appropriate areas of change through which the new institution could be made useful to bring about expected results in transforming the rural society in the years to come. Every reader has to bear in mind that this study does not look at the changes from the perspective of either sanskritization or westernization. The author presents the process of dynamics as such from the perspective of the people.

This study tries to analyse the changes in individuals and institutions in the rural areas in terms of their perception, behaviour and performance. For this study two villages in Dindigul dsistrict were selected. Nariyuthu and Chittaravu were the two villages selected for this work as the two villages had the appropriate characteristics. No structured interview was conducted. Data were gathered from the discussions held in the two villages with the villagers in groups. The discussions were conducted on several days. Elders, youth, women and teachers were involved in the discussions. No specific method or instrument was used to collect data. All available means were used to gather data on transformation and entitlement.

There is yet another interesting area for investigation, namely ensuring entitlement of the people. The State has its own unalterable responsibilities which are to be discharged under any condition. In the course of fifty years, how has the State discharged its basic responsibilities in ensuring the entitlements of the people? This is a question probed in this study by conducting an intensive interview with the people in four villages. From this analysis one can understand the efficacy of the State in India.

One section of this study presents the perception of the researcher while the two preceding chapters are only the reflections of the rural masses without any comment or explanation or interpretation.

Finally, the researcher's major question was, "Where we are heading towards?" To answer this question the researcher has analysed the prevailing conditions and tried to predict what will be the future of life in the rural areas in the first two decades of the twenty-first century.

2

TRANSFORMATION NOW AND THEN

People in the villages join together in many places from dawn to dusk. They meet in the tea stall in the morning, in the paddy field or in the farm house, in the market and in a number of other places. They interact with each other and exchange ideas on a variety of matters from family issues to international affairs. Whenever they find leisure time, they meet and discuss. Topics of discussion vary from group to group. To spend their leisure time they assemble either in the temple premises or in the premises of the *chavadi* (*chavadi* is a public place where people meet). For the specific purpose of collecting data for this work, people were asked to assemble in the premises of panchayat office. The group members assembled at the premises of the gram panchayat office. As the *chavadi* had now been converted into a temple, the elders who used to spend their idle time in the *chavadi* could not find any place other than the Gram Panchayat office. The elders who once held respect and status in the society are losing their importance and it was obvious from their observations in the discussions. The elders mostly while away the time in the panchayati office. Now the panchayat office is a centre for dissemination of information among the public.

Streets and Roads

They stated that the streets were wide enough to accommodate two bullock carts at a time in those days. Now-a-days the breadth of several streets has been narrowed and the space has been encroached for petty shops on both sides of the streets and roads. Very few roads were properly maintained in the villages. There were three kinds of roads, namely mud road, metal road and black topped road. The roads were not in proper condition. Only bullock carts can be used. The surface of roads was not good enough to use four wheelers. Moreover, the roads and streets were not provided with proper lighting facilities. In some of the important places kerosene lights were provided every night and they were managed by the community itself.

But now the streets and roads are either metal or black topped. In Tamil Nadu almost all the rural roads have been made metal roads. Main roads and streets have been provided with street lights. Even the remote corners are provided with electrified street lights.

Drainage

The drainage system was not pucca in the olden days. But the streams and inlet and outlet systems were not disturbed. The ups and downs were quite clear and so the drainage during the rainy days was free and there was no stagnation of water and hence there was no problem. But, at present, there are stagnant pools of water everywhere not only during the rainy days but also in normal days. The people have disturbed the natural flow of streams, by creating ups and downs. So the villagers are facing serious problems due to stagnation of water everywhere. In the name of development construction has been encouraged by the government. All these constructions have obstructed the natural arrangement.

Open-air Toilets

In the past, sites were earmarked as 'manthai' for defecation. Moreover, the size of the population was not so large as we have now. Hence environmental sanitation was not at all a problem in those days. The cattle were also allowed to graze only in the pastures, not in the streets. Grassy pastures were available in every village and they were earmarked for the use of the cattles of the village. But today there is no authority to control the 'manthai'.

Either it has been encroached upon for dumping manure/waste or for house construction by several poor families. Due to this encroachment, the people defecate in and around the village living area and they pollute the environment of the entire village. People in the rural areas are not aware of the implications of open air defecation. People have been oriented in using cosmetics, but they are not oriented in basic sanitation and hygiene.

Sanitation

For toilets people used only the open common grounds and for bathing they used the tanks and wells of the community. Tanks and wells available in different parts of the villages and they were earmarked for different communities. All those tanks and wells were managed by the users as community. But, gradually, these common properties lost their value as people started using water from the overhead tanks provided by the government. Now people, both rich and poor have encroached upon the common properties. Roads are used by the people as toilets. They collect water from public taps, and use it in the premises of the house for bathing. Individual toilets and community toilets have been provided and yet people are not oriented to use the toilets. In the villages there were small pits in every house to dump all the wastes in and they became organic manure for agriculture. Now there is no such practice. All waste material are dumped abroad indiscriminately. One can find a mixture of biodegradable and non-biodegradable material in the waste. All the waste lies in the street and is not removed. Villages are now virtually dung heaps and mounds of non-biodegradable wastes. Once streets were clean, household waste was preserved to be converted into organic manure. People had a clear cut idea about each and everything that they saw and dealt with everyday. Till date little serious attempt has been made to create awareness about the importance of sanitation. This is a neglected area. People had not been made to realise the importance of sanitation and hence this degradation. It is clear that the condition of sanitation in the rural areas has moved from bad to worse despite many attempts on the part of the government through its programmes.

Food Habit

A variety of grains were the food items in those days. Sorghum, ragi, kampu and other millets were the major food items. People used to take food after a course of labour not early in the morning. The second meal was only at late evening. They took food only twice a day. Some people ate green gram/bengal gram or groundnut in the evening as snacks. Only the rich, had the practice of drinking coffee or milk. But the food items were rich in nutrition. Greens, *dhal,* oil and grains like ragi and sorghum were full of protein, vitamins and fat. Hence, they did not suffer from illness frequently. At present they take tiffin in the morning, rice and vegetable for lunch as well as supper. Rarely they take sorghum or ragi. Banana was the only fruit commonly available in those days. Now, orange, grapes, guava, pineapple, papaya, mango and sappota are the fruits available to the villagers. But due to the cost of vegetables, the villagers are now using vegetables limitedly. And also due to the changing of cropping pattern, the various types of grams are not produced in the village. Hence the intake of cereals is limited.

In general the food items has rich nutritive value in those days. Now the people are aware of the nutritive value of food in taken. But everything is calculated in rupees, which means the purchasing power of the people. The increase of other consuming needs has its own impact on the food expenditure now. People in those days had the habit of taking cereals as their food. They did not know the value of vegetables but they took the vegetables available at hand. Whatever, was cheap was consumed by the people. Most people used to grow some plants to get vegetables for their daily use. Their life was oriented to taking whatever was available. Their life style was shaped by nature. Food was secured to each individual by the community. People never purchased food material from outside the village. Sometimes they brought food material through exchange of ragi and millet and they formed their daily diet. Rice was considered status symbol thirty years back. Rice was served once in a while when they celebrated any function in the family. Moreover, it was considered a luxury and a rich man's diet. The

Green Revolution brought rice not only to the districts which grow rice but also to all the districts. Slowly people were oriented to taking rice regularly. Ragi and millet are not considered regular food material now. People take ragi and millet only when they are prescribed by the doctor. Drinking coffee, tea, cool drinks and taking snacks in the snack bar and hotels are common at present. People have been trained to take such beverages. In those days people took only water from ragi or millet soaked overnight. Just like taking tea, they used to consume this water. Snack bars or tea stalls were not common in those days in the villages. Only one or two tea stalls functioned in a village. Women never had the practice of taking food in the hotels in those days. Now governments are making a sincere effort to create awareness about the nutritive value of the food which we take. But in those days, without knowing all this detailed information about the nature of food, people took certain varieties of food which had rich nutritive value needed for the human body. Almost all of them were non-vegetarians. Brahmins were exceptional. Importance was attached to non-vegetarian varieties of food.

Costumes

No serious attention was paid to the dress in those days. Children and adults had only two to three sets of dress. They used to buy *banians* and trousers for children and *dhoti kada* for adults. Wearing towel was not practised by everyone. They did not see silk clothes. The clothes were purchased at the weekly market. No purchase was made in the event of any celebrations. Clothes were purchased only when needed.

The women took care to cover their body. The *sari* was sixteen feet long. There was no practice of wearing blouse or brassier or *petticoat* in those days. The lengthy saree was enough to cover their chest and back properly. The saris were purely of cotton. Only the *kuraipattu* known as the wedding sari was a little bit attractive in the border and in its colour. Now-a-days the material and pattern have drastically changed. Polyester, silk, spun and kodusilk are the various dress materials of women of all the age groups and everyone of them is wearing a blouse. The adult women go in for various patterns of blouses low cut, long neck, etc. Readymade brassiers are used by them. They use *petticoats* also. Some women are used to wearing undergarment (readymade panties) also. Some women take along some other dress while going for labour work. After their work is over, they switch over to the normal dress. The group respondents complained that now-a-days the dress draws much attention among the women. They do not worry about their gender speciality. Their dress habit is now posing a problem to every head of the family in the village. Whenever a new style or variety is introduced, the women are inclined to purchase those types of clothes in addition to the usual dress material during the festival season.

In earlier days the clothes were purchased only by the male members of the family. At present women are not even taking men along with them for the purchase. Also colour matching was not known to them in those days. Now it is strictly followed. The wedding sari has become a very important item and its cost varies from Rs. 2000 to Rs. 30,000 and, even in a poor family, people purchase silk saris for a wedding. Wearing of jewels in gold as well as imitation studs, chains, rings has now become common. In earlier days only elderly women used to have an elongated ear sporting a earring of a special type. Other women wore ear and nose stud only. Now purchasing of jewels and silver anklets in a very common practice even among poor families. The new awareness of youth (women and men) in matters of dress, beautification and style are all due to the entry of film, TV and other media.

Social Activities

Social control was perpetuated by the caste system in the rural areas. The caste leaders' opinions and suggestions were strictly adhered to in those days. The law enforcing authorities were the higher caste group leaders and they established social controls over the individuals who indulged in anti-social activities like distilling and selling illicit liquor, rowdyism and gambling. The teaching community was respected by the villagers and they properly advised the erring adult members in the community.

At present the caste control is not so rigid as in the earlier days. The adults are not respected by the elders. The political activities of various groups make them feel independent. The police in general are not able to control the anti-social elements in the rural areas. Sometime they join hands with anti-social elements also.

Social unity was in order in those days. Maintenance of public tanks, wells, temple sites were undertaken collectively by the people. Drinking water was available in all seasons in all wells, because of the management system adopted by the community. Now most of the wells are dry. The taste of the water is not good. Borewells are available in many houses. Public service is not recognised. Laziness is in everybody's mind. The people did not wait for the panchayat to do any welfare work in those days. Now everybody is expecting that the panchayat would do welfare activities.

Religious Activities

Temple celebration was one of the most important social activities. All caste groups joined together and participated in the celebrations. People used to wear costumes of different characters from the puranas and participate in folk dances and drama. They uses to sing, dance, *bharatam* and climb *kalumaram* (which was polished so well that the climber slipped down) and sprinkle yellow coloured water on others. These activities gave opportunities to youth to show their talents and skills. In course of time, these celebrations were replaced by modern theatrical activities with the help of outside agencies. Dance by outsiders, light music troupe, record dance, 16 mm film and TV film are the items of entertainment now. People had nurtured different cultural programmes with the active participation of the people and now professional artists, groups have replaced all those evolved cultural programmes of the people. Though the cultural programmes were owned by the communities, each caste group having its own special art and programme, when the programmes were performed in public places, they were respected by the people and they were not witnessed from the perspective of the caste hierarchy. But now the conditions are different. The youths have cultivated exclusive caste feelings and do not mingle freely with the other caste youths during the temple celebrations. The practice of considering the other caste group as relatives by calling them 'uncle', 'cousin or sister' has now faded away. Only the elders still continue to use these relationships. The youths are not known to maintain this type of relationship. In the villages youths were organised in groups and they played games like swimming, climbing trees and kabadi but those games are now-a-days not in practice. They play cricket. School children are learning cycling.

The youth did not have money in those days. Now they get money. They work and earn money. Many are in business. So money transaction is more now and they have developed the habit of alcoholism, smoking, *ganja* (selling locally), watching blue films and involving in prostitution. The elders feel that these are the result of the material developments achieved in the village. The material development has not developed social living. Instead, it has dragged the people into anti-social activities.

Life was very hard to lead in those days. Life's needs were not many. They did not murmur over the difficulties they had faced. At present life comforts have increased. There are several avenues to earn money from farming, business, trade, estate work, government employment, private employment, tea shops and petty shops.

Marriage

Horoscope and caste rituals played a predominant role in marriages in the village. The rituals varied from caste to caste in the same village. Village elders, caste leaders, village leaders, chieftains had been in the functioned as presiding leaders at marriages. The function was spread over about five to six days. The function was well regulated. The wedding function was conducted either in the house itself or in the temples. The bridegroom was dressed as a king and he was brought to the place of the function on a horse in a procession and both men and women participated in the procession. Series of rituals were conducted from the first day to the last. The rituals widely varied from caste to caste. Prayers were conducted in the local temples. To mark the wedding ceremony a variety of cultural programmes were arranged by cultural troupes from the same village. The cultural troupes exhibited their talents in front of the leaders of the community and village. Folk songs were sung by the folk artists. A variety of gifts had to be given to the couple. Widows were not permitted to remarry. Intercaste marriage was not permitted. Nobody attempted these in the village because the community had its own control over the families and individuals. The marriage functions were conducted only during the nights. To distinguish the married women from the unmarried, married women were asked to have a kumkum mark on the forehead and wear a *toe-thing*.

Marriage was considered a solemn ceremony with values. It was conducted within the framework established by the community based on the cherished values evolved over the years. During all the five days, rituals were carried out as per the direction of the elders of the community who were designated as *pujaris* for this specific occasion. Close relatives were the participants on all the five days. Marriages were conducted only during the summer as there was no work for the people then. It was a convention or a custom that the bridegroom had to offer jewels to the bride. It was not in bargain. The quantum of jewels to be offered to the bride would indicate the economic and social status of the family of the bridegroom. A variety of dishes were prepared and served on all the five days. During these functional days, there would be mutual cooperation among various social groups to conduct the function. Barber, *dobhi,* carpenter, *purohith*, potter and a number of others used to partake in the function to share responsibilities earmarked for them and they were equally rewarded through some economic benefits given by the family which conducted the function. It was a joyful event not only for the newly wedded couple but also for all the close relatives of the couple. From the day of marriage to the day of Consummation (first night) they (the couple) had to perform a variety of rituals and they were allowed to move freely with each other and get acquainted with each other in temperament. An auspicious was fixed for their conjugal union. The newly married couple had to visit several holy places to seek the blessings of the divine for their marital life. Caste was so rigid and likewise clan was also maintained. Inter-caste and inter-religions marriages were unheard of during those days. Marriages were arranged only among close relatives. In some families even at childhood they used to decide who was for whom. Very rarely they went in for alliance with a distant relative.

In some communities, there was a community stipulation that they should not go beyond close relatives. If anybody wanted to go beyond close relatives, they had to seek the permission of the community by paying some amount of money fixed by the community. Parents of the girl used to start the process of seeking alliance immediately after she attained puberty. Girls got married at the age of thirteen and fourteen and, at the maximum at fifteen. Boys got married before they attained the age of twenty. The rituals were carried out only through the elders of the community. Families spent money depending upon their economic and social status. During the function, close relatives were given gifts in the form of cloth and other materials mostly durables. Hence they had to spend a lot. There were families who spent beyond their level of economy to keep up their social status and thereby lost their economic status. Parents used to search for brides only through temple festivals or through women belonging to the *dobhi* community or through some elders who had been performing this assignment for several decades.

At present marriages are conducted mostly in marriage halls in the nearby towns. Only the poor conduct them in the village itself. Rigidity of marrying close relatives has been given the go-by. The primary consideration while fixing the marriage is money and material. The State has enabled the families to go beyond the control of the community system. By and large people maintain their caste system for their cultural identity. The concept of marriage among relatives has gone. It is not considered so value based. Rituals are not adhered so strictly. All kinds of rituals have been compressed and shorter versions have been introduced. People have been oriented to look at the whole affair from the perspective of the economy of the concerned individual and the family. Mostly marriage functions are conducted in one single day. It will stretch not more than a day. Unlike in the olden days, before finalising the alliance the bride and the bridegroom are consulted and their opinion is also considered if they are valuable. The interference of the elders in the marriage has been reduced considerably. During those days costumes were in the traditional form. Rarely the functions were photographed. But now costumes are in the western form. The entire function is videographed irrespective of the economic status. The rituals have been commercialised since for each and every ritual, money value is given. The parents of the bridegroom and he himself expect monetary benefit from the bride's father or mother whether they are financially sound or not. During the olden days, they had no such monetary expectation. A marriage in a family was considered a function of the community. Close relatives of the family would contribute their mite either in cash or in kind. As a token of love, presents would be given in cash. It signified the bondage between and among families. Attendance of the relatives at the function was perceived only through this presentation which was popularly called *mohimai* or *moi.* It was considered an essential duty of everyone to participate in the function. Now it has been totally changed. It is an affair of an individual family. Sometimes, even within the family, it is an affair of the particular individual concerned.

Generally early marriage is avoided now. The difference of age between bride and bridegroom is not so wide as in earlier days. Illiterate working girls' (casual labourers') marriages are arranged before the age of 18 to 19. The parents fear about the possibility of their character being spoilt as they have to interact with men in the work spot. There is no protection for them. Earlier the caste distinction was strictly adhered to and hence there was no worry about the occurrence of inter-caste marriages.

Celebrations now seem to be a mere show to display the status of the family. Customary practices during the marriage celebrations are now not known to the community concerned. Unique practices are forgotten and most of the marriage celebrations are prototype. For the convenience of relatives and local people, sometimes the marriages are arranged in the evenings in those days. If the bride is a distant relative, the parents voluntarily offer dowry. If the bridegroom employed, the family of the bride is ready to contribute money towards marriage day feast expenses. Middle class people among the Pillai, Servai and Naicker caste are engaging Brahmin Purohithar to perform marriages even today.

In general, employing a brahman purohith during the 16th day celebration to baptise the new born babies, house warming ceremony, function at the time of girls attaining puberty and new business inauguration has increased recently.

Only poor families are taking brides from among their close relatives. The rich do not prefer close relatives. They select brides from among the distant relatives or total strangers. Rituals are now being limited due to the hurried life style. Even close relatives are leaving the marriage house/hall on the same day. They avoid staying for longer duration. Among the SC community still the community leader is the VIP during the marriage celebration. The practice of demanding of ring, watch, minor chain for the bridegroom is in practice among the upper middle class at present. In the SC Christian community, the marriages are conducted in very simple form. The religious head is the important person in the function. Even uneducated bridegrooms are demanding watch and ring now. Inviting friends from other communities for marriage celebration is considered proof of as social status. Marriage celebrations are organised as public meetings. Presidential address, felicitations, gift presentation are the common items on the agenda. Household articles like vessels, cot, fan, TV, mixer, grinder are expected as items of dowry. Business people expect cash as dowry from brides.

The rituals like *nalungu* and *nalseivathu* are arranged on different day by different group of relatives. Now, within an hour, on the eve of the marriage, all rituals are arranged in the marriage hall itself. At present, even after the marriage, customs like inviting the couple for Aadi, Diwali celebration are in practice in many middle class families. Celebration of marriage day is a new arrival among middle class families. The practice of singing songs by women members during marriage celebration is now not in practice. There is no harmonious relationship among the relatives. Hence most of them prefer to have marriage alliance with families not related to them. Moreover, they prefer outside marriage as they cannot demand dowry from close relatives. Now money is considered the major determinant factor in deciding the relationship between and among individuals.

Engaging van, taxi, bus is at present a practice in marriage celebration. Family deity was considered as the main god during the celebration in those days. Now the rituals before the family deity are limited. The offering of food to the deity and performing pooja are now limited and sometimes not practised at all.

Bringing the dowry items in a vehicle is considered proof of social status. Taking the dowry items during the marriage procession is also a new culture. While fixing the bridegroom, mostly close relatives were consulted in those days. Now their views are not taken seriously. Verification of the income and employment of the bridegroom is the main consideration at present. But, in those days, the bridegroom's behaviour, conduct and character were verified with so many people.

Political party affiliation becomes one of the major factors for social interaction and, so, during marriage, the friends are drawn from their own party and other political parties. In a small village within a short span of time about eight inter-caste marriages have been conducted but not openly. Almost all the marriages were celebrated outside and the couples returned to the village only after two or three years. Printing of felicitation posters, erecting arches for the marriage, distribution of felicitation cards by friends are now in common practice. Mike set, loudspeaker, stereo boxes, colour serial light, a number of tube lights, decorative pandals are the celebration items during the marriage day. During the marriage celebration, the friends of the bridegroom join together and they take alcoholic drinks and the dinner expenses are met by the bridegroom.

Among Muslims, it is reported that the female population is more and hence they are arranging early marriages. The bride's parents are ready to give handsome dowry to a deserving bridegroom. The rituals and other celebrations are arranged only in the evening. For one poor Muslim marriage, the Muslim community committee collected donation and a dowry of Rs. 10,000 was given along with some jewels. Due to dowry demand, marriages between close relatives are again realised. To meet the dowry expenses, the parents are selling their properties like land, housesite and jewels. Puberty celebration is now considered proof of a social status.

Dress and Cosmetics

Thirty years back importance was not attached to dress material. Only a pair of dress material for each individual was available. Quality of dress material varied from family to family. Young men had the practice of wearing *dothi* and shirt. Old men who had crossed the age of forty did not wear any shirt. Women folk had not developed the habit of purchasing more dress material. They were interested in acquiring wealth in the form of gold or cash or land. Moreover the dress material was designed so attractively as it is now.

Now people have developed a taste for possessing more number of dress materials. Even in the rural areas, modern dress materials like *chudidar, salvar-kamiz,* and nighty are commonly used by the young girls. Women irrespective of their age, wear silk *saris*. Dress materials are so attractive in design. The fashion of the dress material is being shaped by the cinema. People spend a lot on dress. During those days of history people mostly relied on the services of the *dhobi* to wash their dress. But now, due to proliferation of a variety of washing detergent powders and cakes, people wash their dress material on their own. Dress material are given to *dhobi* only for ironing.

People now, irrespective of age, gender, caste and income use cosmetics. People in those days did not use soap, shampoo, talcum powder, cream and scent. They had not developed a taste for using these items of cosmetics. Dress materials are mostly polyester now. Dress materials of cotton are now considered low status symbols among the middle class and the poor.

Now readymade garments, pants and shirts in new styles and patterns are purchased in cities and towns. Even elderly women prefer to wear polyester saris. Due to its transparency, they wear petticoat also now. Undergarments were once stitched in tailoring shops. Now the women are purchasing readymade ones. Men also purchase readymade garments. Wearing of pants and full shirt is considered as a status symbol now. Not only during festival times, whenever they wish, women and men purchase new clothes. Single fold *dhothi* is now used by elders only. Most adults wear double fold polyester *dhothi*. Wearing of silk *dhothi* even after marriage is considered a status symbol. People are attracted towards dress. Earlier once a month the *dhobi* take soiled clothes for washing. Now everywhere self wash is practised as detergent powders and cakes are available. Only for ironing people give their clothes to the *dhobi*. New types of dress material like polyester, terycotton, spun are easy to wash and maintain and hence people have developed a preference for the new material. Purchasing clothes from street vendors is now not in practice. Only very poor families rely on street vendors. As family members earn individually they themselves purchase their clothes whenever they wish from nearby towns. Even villagers are going to tours like Dindigul/Madurai for purchasing clothes.

Women now give importance to getting matching clothes and stylish blouses of cotton mixed with ployester. The sari size is now reduced. Old fashioned long size, cotton saris for elders are not available in cloth shops at present. Muslim women use *purdah* and for this they spend a lot as decoration is now costly. Girls are wearing *chudidar.* Elders have given up the practice of domming a towel on their shoulders. Womenfolk now give importance to the colour and the border of the *saris*. Elders, especially the men have developed a taste for polyester shirts.

Habit of Using Footwear

People have developed the habit of using *chappals*. They choose only modern variety of *chappals* and shoes. Youths wear shoes during important functions. Local cobbler services are not for making new *chappals*. They are attending to repair work only. In the past none except a few had the practice of wearing *chappals* or shoes. Hair clipping was done in order to remove the excess hair. Now it has becomes hair dressing. Everyday shave was unheard of during those days. But now it has become the practice. Only old men shave their face once in a week. All youths shave their face everyday. Mostly the youths are being influenced by the cinema. New hair styles are based on the impact of movies. There is no correlation between the income and expenditure. A major portion of the income of the poor goes for alcoholic drinks, cosmetics, tobacco and lottery tickets. Men wear 'minor' chain, chain, and bracelet on wrist, made of gold.

Service of Barber

Barbers used to visit the houses frequently to attend the needs of the family members. There was working arrangement between the household and the barber. Every year the barber use to get a lump compensation for the work done throughout the year. Mostly he got it in kind not in cash, in the form of grains. Now no barber is willing to serve in the rural areas as it is not profitable. Hence they have migrated from the rural areas to urban centres. Using cosmetics like soap, shampoo, talcum powder, sprays, paste, cream and ornaments are common among the people irrespective of their economic status. The rich and the poor use cosmetics.

Facilities

Medical Facilities

Delivering a baby at home is considered as unsafe. Yet, due to poverty, there is no other way excepting relying on the traditional *dais.* The native *dai* suggests a hospital delivery if it is necessary. The practice of post-natal care in those days was mainly based on the traditional medicines prepared at home. The practice of keeping the wife away from the husband for three months after delivery is now not strictly adhered to. Awareness of pre-natal care is generated and women are demanding regular visits of ANMs at present. The practice of the *dai* visiting every week, attending to child care services like oil bathing, etc., is also in vogue. Men are now evincing keen interest in knowing the health status of pregnant women. Once it was considered the job exclusive of women. Homeo and *Siddha* medical practices are now not considered for practice by villagers. The hereditary home prepared medicines are unknown to the present generation. For everything people rely on allopathic medicines. Uneducated poor women do not go for pre-natal check-up in the hospitals though the facilities are available in the hospitals. Around one-third of the rural populace are still unaware of modern ideas in respect of child rearing. Post-natal care including strict diet, self-control, and using native medicines was in practice in those days. People relied completely on the home system of preparing medicine for treating the patients. There was no common formula to prepare those medicines. There were *siddha* doctors in the rural areas. In those days people believed only in God in the absence of a proven system of medicine. Donkey's milk was fed to a newborn baby in those days. At present allopathic medical treatment to children is preferred even by villagers.

Yet another practice people developed in the rural areas in those days was that, whenever any member of the family fell sick, special prayer were conducted before the family deity. Intensity of prayer depended on the nature of the disease affecting the individual. There were many practices which were traditional in nature to maintain health by using different kinds of oil. Slowly people have lost their interest and faith in them as preparation of the oil takes time to heel the body. From each and every street or hamlet one family was dedicated to preparing country medicine in those days. It was not a business but a service for which a nominal service charge was fixed. In some places the family was attached to a temple and hence the whole amount charged for this service was given to the temple. Medicinal plants were grown in the gardens of the temple. A variety of medicines were prepared and administered, but there was no record for all those medicines other than oral history. Adequate care was given to the children by the elders in those days in the families. But, now one cannot expect such care in agricultural families. People prefer only nuclear family. Hence they are sending them to balwadi/nursery school. In one village three nursery schools are being run by private individuals. Two government aided balwadis are there. School going children are practising cycling. Cricket is preferred by adolescent boys in this village. Girls also practice cycling.

There was no formal recreation in those days. A few traditional games were played by the youth in the villages. Deepawali is now gaining importance. Spending on dress during festival season is more now. Spending huge amounts of money on crackers, cinema, alcoholic drinks and tour for Deepawali is normal. Rituals during family deity celebrations are now limited. Grand celebration to family deity is not being arranged due to migration of relatives to other areas and due to non-availability of money also.

Caste-wise temple celebration/administration is in practice still. Record dance, drama, rural sports etc., are the different items during temple celebration today. Inviting friends during family deity celebration is a new trend in the villages. Alagar Temple celebration was the common festival in which all communities use to participate. Even Muslims used to give donation. Now huge amounts are fixed as individual family contribution towards temple celebration, for which people borrow money at interest. The celebration is now extended from three to seven days. It was a one-day affair earlier. Video film, 16 mm film, light music with dance are the new items introduced in celebrations. Youths used to participate in the religious functions. Youth used to contribute money and provide programmes in the functions of the festival in those days. Now they don't have faith in these activities and they have lost their interest also. Youth are coming forward to take leadership in celebration. Festivals were conducted on mutual cooperation among the caste groups earlier but now there are too many differences among the collectivities during celebration and sometimes, this leads to social tension and conflict. Celebrations are now meant to show one's image and status. Earlier it was conducted for spiritual development and human unity.

School

Earlier a school was organised at a mosque. In course of time it became a religious school. During the earlier part of the 19th century, Christian missionaries came and organised a school. It is still functioning. It is a primary school. The infrastructure facilities are not sufficient. Most of the time, the classes were organised under the trees. The panchayat union is also running a school. At present the school has classes up to the eighth standard. It is being run with government grant, and it has got good building facilities. An indisciplined headmaster in the school for a long period and now a lady headmistress has been appointed and the old headmaster was transferred to another school, due to local body initiatives. There are two balwadis run by the government in the same village. There are two nursery schools being run by a private management.

The people feel that every school must be provided with adequate facilities like building, playground, classroom, educational equipments and that the students must be encouraged to participate in extracurricular activities. At present they demand that the school must be upgraded into a high school or higher secondary school. Only rich people can send their children to nearby matriculation schools to continue their studies. The girls are not able to continue their studies after the 8th standard in the village. Once education for women was totally neglected. The middle income group families are able to send their children to Pattiveerran patti, a nearby town area for high school studies. The poor cannot send their children there after 8th standard. Teachers are changing their lethargic attitude and engage classes properly due to the intervention of local bodies. Children are coming regularly bringing books and notes and dressed neatly. Cleanliness must be taught to all school children. The people sincerely recollect their old days when they struggled to educate a few from their village by sending them to a school which was far away from their village. In fifty years the government has provided facilities to the people, especially in the field of education. The schools might not have adequate facilities and care may not be taken to maintain the school properly. But some facilities have been provided and the people admit that they do not know the strategy to maintain the facilities provided by the government. They feel that the absence of local body institutions has driven the people away from the government. They further feel that before the government took the initiative to provide the educational facilities, the missionaries took steps to start a school and hence religious institutions have a better hold over the people than the governmental institution.

Communication

Initially a post office was used only to send communication to far-away places. Later the people came to know of the other facilities. Now knowledge of Savings Account at Post Office has been enhanced. Scheduled caste families are also opening Savings Bank accounts and purchasing Indira Vikas Patras etc. People have developed the practice of using the post office for communication facilities. Now the practice of sending letters to distant places has fallen as telephone facilities have increased. STD facility is available and used by villagers. People have realised the importance of STD facility and demand STD facilities for villages. Traders contact merchants of Dindigul and verify the prices of various agriculture products in the weekly market. All modern communication facilities are used by the people in the villages irrespective of their educational background.

Transportation

For the employment opportunity in the hills, a large number of poeple are using the bus facilities to reach the hills. The frequency in the morning is limited. Hence they have requested the authorities of the state transport corporation for additional bus services. As the unreserved forests are now-a-days under cultivation by private people, they request road services upto their area so as to transport their produce to markets easily. They have replied that the existing road is now under encroachment. It has to be cleared. They also report that, after 8.00 p.m., bus services from Dindigul to Sitharevu is not available. They need services up to 9.30 p.m. During the olden days there were no such facilities. The bullock cart was the only vehicle. People rarely visited cities and towns. Farmers used to go to towns to purchase material and to sell their agricultural products. They used only bullock carts. Petty traders also visited the towns and cities to purchase articles for sale in the villages. One would find more number of bullock carts in the villages in those days. When activities were not mechanised, every individual was totally involved in anyone activity in the village in one form or the other. Moreover, there were no road facilities to use motor vehicles. In most of the places agricultural products were shifted from one place to another in headloads. Human drudgery was visible everywhere. People were trained to carry heavy headloads of material. But at present people do not have any such training. Human drudgery has been reduced drastically by providing adequate facilities. The elders feel that the government has provided enough to the community but the community has not kept all those facilities in proper use.

Drainage

In those days the topography of the village was not disturbed. Now the drainage is not organised properly. There was no indiscriminate construction at all places in those days. Even wherever houses were built, they were in topographical order without any disturbance to the natural system of drainage. But, at present there is no logic or reason as to where houses are to be constructed. As a result, the natural flow path has been obstructed and the artificial drainage systems are not properly maintained.

Now they demand a large type of drainage, deep enough to drain out the water wherever it stagnates. Every lane has to be provided with proper drainage, the people feel. At the road side the drainage is now natural. Now people demand side construction and also small bridges to the dwelling area which have come up then recently.

People have discontinued the habit of keeping a clean environment. People then had a wise way of maintaining environmental conditions. Vast stretches of lands were earmarked as grazing ground and in every village one would find lands with thick bushes and those lands were used as toilets by the community. These lands were away from the habitat area. Moreover, people grew cattle in large numbers and hence they earmarked a separate place for the cattle. Agricultural waste and waste accumulated in houses were deposited in a pit and made into organic manure which was used for their farming operations. Thus houses, streets and public places were clean. But now the situation is different. Cattle have been reduced to a minimum number and they are always in sites very near to the houses. They don't move out as there is no grazing land and all the grazing land has been encroached upon. And also the waste materials are now mixed with having plastic polythene bags, broken bottles, tins, and save other bio-non-degradable materials which do not drain out and block the way. Earlier the bathing and washing was done at tanks and wells outside the houses. Now everything is done at home. Hence more waste water has to be drained out.

Water Supply

People now demand individual house tap connection. About 100 families have borewell at their house sites. The wells dug earlier are not maintained now. The community feeling and common actions like digging of wells, maintaining the same by the concerned street youth happened only in those days. Now-a-days they feel it is the duty of the panchayat. The electric motor is frequently under repair. The main well is accessible only to people other than the SC community. The tanks and ponds were once used for bathing and washing. Now they are empty. The washing of most clothes is done only in the house. Hence more water is drained out into the street. In those days the people installed sewage pit/soak pit by their own labour but now there are open drains on the streets. At present the government is providing drinking water supply to the people. In some places they provide hand pumps and in a few places they provide overhead tanks. It is not clear to what extent people are satisfied with the facilities. To what extent all those facilities are utilised by the people is a major question raised by the elders of the villages. As long as water was taken from hand pump it was clean and protected. But now water is stored in the tank and released through a pipe line. An overhead tank has to be maintained properly. Otherwise it will supply only polluted water. They feel that there is no match between the people's need and the schemes of the government.

Road

Footpaths, lanes and minor roads were used by the people in those days to move from one place to another. It was normal for the sides of the lanes, footpaths and roads to have shade giving trees. Human settlements were away from the roads. Tamarind and mango trees on the roadside yielded fruits to the tune of several lakhs of rupees to the panchayats. The roads and lanes in the villages are now encroached upon. The main road is also encroached upon by private shops (The P.W.D. officials and revenue officials collect illegally an amount as rent from the encroachers). There is no passenger's waiting shed on the roadside. Every place is encroached upon by private persons. Maintenance work on roads is rarely carried out. People demand metal roads in their villages.

Hospital

Ten years back, with the help and guidance of Gandhigram Trust (Kasthurba Hospital) a Health Centre was started by the village committee. The trainee doctors regularly visited Sitharevu Health Centre and treated the people. This arrangement was discontinued as there was no visit of trainee doctors. Then the government built a Health Sub-centre. The nurse is not staying at the centre. Dates of her visit are not known to the villagers. The sub-centre is now used by gamblers, as there is no door to protect the verandah. There are three homeopathy doctors. They give injection also. Only one doctor from Pattiveeranpatti comes daily evening for one hour. He leaves quickly as he has another clinic at Pattiveeranpatti. Recently one medical store was opened. People usually go to Pattiveeranpatti, Batlagundu or Dindigul for medical treatment. They demand a fullfledged hospital. (But as per the government guidelines a hospital is meant for a population of about 30,000). Out of the three homeopathy doctors, two are from outside. The *siddha* practitioners are not receiving encouragement. They also visit villages rarely. Only on order they prepare and administer *siddha* medicines. Before Independence there was no such medical facility. Only the traditional medical practitioners took care of the people.

Now facilities are abundant in different places and communication facilities are also available to reach all the places where these facilities are available. Now people need money to make use of these facilities. Institutions established by the government have not been properly maintained and people do not have faith in those institutions. People do not have money, and they have to rely on those facilities provided by the government.

Electrification

Giving power supply to the rural areas is a major progamme of the government. In those days, people never dreamt of such facilities. None had the facility. After seven o'clock there was no movement in the villages because there was no lighting facility. Now everywhere street lights are on. Even a small house has a bulb. About 1000 houses have electrification out of 2500 houses. Street lights are not properly maintained. New street lights are needed at new residential areas coming up on the Ayyampalayam road as well as Thandikudi Hills road. Out of 120 street lights only 30 to 40 are in operation.

Market

There is no weekly or other type of market at Sitharevu. People used to go to Ayyampalayam and Pattiveeranpatti, Batlagundu and Sempatti markets. Vegetables are transported to Oddanchatiram market. There are a large number of trader's commission agents, locally available, who deal with agricultural products marketing—jaggery, sorghum, paddy, cotton, chilly, vegetables, coconut, hill products like pepper, coffee, banana, jackfruit. The cattle traders are in large number. They used to purchase cattle in and around villages and keep them for sale. About twenty traders are earning a lot through this cattle trade. Nearby and far away villagers are regularly visiting Sitharevu to buy cattle. They prefer this type of purchase than at *weekly sandai* (market). Now it is informed that there is trade in the weekly market too.

Ayyampalayam	Mondays	Vegetables/Provision
Sempatti	Fridays	Cattle
Batlagundu	Daily	Vegetables/Provision
Tharmathupatti	Tuesdays	Vegetables/Provision
Nilakkottai	Saturdays	Sheep/Goat/Vegetables
Ottanchathiram	Daily	Vegetables

Community Hall

There is no community hall. A common place available at the Muthalamman temple site is now converted into a temple mandapam. Since there is no necessity to get permission to sit in the mandapam, it is converted into a common place to meet and chat for all the people. The verandah of panchayat office is now utilised as a common place, where the elders sit and chat. The Mooper Community Mutharayar Sangam purchased a land site and initiated the construction of a community hall. People demand that a community hall can be built by the panchayat and its income as rent can be added to the panchayat revenue. The Government must give a loan to *caste sangam* (legally constituted) for the construction of a community hall.

Financial Institution

About a group of ten individuals are involved in financing. Roughly five lakhs of rupees have been the turn over, they said. The rate of interest is twenty four per cent, despite the fact that there are Nationalised Banks in the towns very near to the villages. Most of the people do not have the practice of making use of the banks. There are cooperative societies where people are beneficiaries and receive benefits. But the cooperative institutions and the banking sector are not willing to give adequate credit facilities to the people who don't have repayment ethics. Hence private money lenders are thriving.

Temple

Temples are the symbol of culture. Temples were constructed by the people through their liberal contributions. Each community has its own temple and they are being maintained and managed by the caste groups. Temple management is a prestige of the community. Families which have got reputation and status in leading the community manage the temples. Periodically renovations have been carried out for which people used to contribute liberally. Very big temples with cast properties have been taken away by the government. The Alagar temple is the only temple under the administrative control of Government's Religious and Endowments Charitable Board. The Alagar temple celebration has been conducted by the people of Pattiveeranpatti. The trustees are from political parties. Hence local community leaders feel that they are not respected even though they have contributed largely to the management of the temple for some-time. The harmony among castes is not as strong as in earlier days. Hence celebrations are now organised to show the superiority of each caste. Most of the temple lands have been encroached upon by the villagers as the temples were not maintained properly. While conducting temple festivals all the villagers invited. Each and every segment will have to perform certain earmarked functions. Hierarchy is being maintained perfectly among the caste groups. The grand festivals of the temple are being conducted mostly in summer. The usual festivals are being conducted during auspicious days. Details of the temple management and period of festivals are given in the following Table.

Temples

Name	*Nature*	*Management*
Muthalamman	Public	Moopar
Alagar Kovil	Public	Government
Chinnamman	Public	Moopar
Dhurgaiamman	Public	Moopar
Ganesa	Public	Servai
Angalaparameshwari	Public	Servai
Kaliamman Kovil	Public	Harijan
Mosque		Jamath
CSI Church-SC Christian	Public	Diocese

Festival Months

Panguni	-	March-April
Aippasi	-	Oct.-Nov.
Purattasi	-	Sep.-Oct.
Chithirai	-	April-May

Irrigation Sources/Channels

About one hundred hectares are under tank irrigation. Around one hundred wells are functioning in the village to cater to the needs of the farmers. The Marudha river dam water is mostly used by Pattiveeranpatti farmers. A canal was built for about ten kilometres. But due to imperfect design, the sidewalls are often damaged and disturb the water flow. One division from the dam is totally diverted for the flow of water to Pattiveeranpatti. The other division is for Sitharevu area. The Pattiveeranpatti farmers do not allow to store water up to the permitted level as they fear that their field/forest would be submerged. Illegally they flush out the water and reduce the storage. This has affected the flow in the second channel earmarked for Sitharevu villages. Tank deepening work has not been done for many years. Generally people in those days relied on small tanks and ponds for the water supply for their small farming operations. The ponds, tanks and wells were under the control of the community. Individual wells were also available. Tanks and ponds were managed by the community very well and water was distributed equitably. To deepen the tanks and ponds the communities took up the responsibility and collected money from the users. People had an efficient system of management of water in those days.

Resources and Facilities

The village has got the following resources:

* Unreserved forest
* Tanks
* Dry land
* Wet land

* Hill estate
* Cattle wealth
* Commission trades
* Human resources
* Cooperative society
* Coir factory
* Library
* Schools
* Informal traders
* Agricultural labour
* Skilled labour — masons, carpenters, blacksmith, mat weavers.

Other Infrastructure

* Panchayat office
* V.A.O. Office
* Primary Agriculture Cooperative Bank
* PAC Sub-centre
* Seven wells (drinking water)
* Water tank
* Government middle school
* CSI Primary School
* Creche (Government)
* Private Nursery School
* Public tap
* Drinking water sources — in two places, borewell + Pump (electrified)

Sitharevu Village Land Details

*	Wetland	479.80.0 acres
*	Dryland	2076.39.0 acres
*	Wasteland	14.26.0 acres
*	Common wetland	2.39.5 acres
*	Common dryland	36.98.5 acres
*	Poromboke	315.91.5 acres
*	Hill dryland	209.37.5 acres

The details given above are to illustrate the facilities and resources available in the village. It is a major question whether all the facilities provided to the people are properly maintained by the community or utilised by the people for their development. Well informed individuals had utilised all the opportunities for their development. School was organised but it is not properly managed and the same is not utilised by the community for its advantages. Medical facilities have been provided and yet they are not utilised and, instead, people are searching for private doctors. Communication facilities have been provided and they are also not utilised by the people. In the villages it is strongly felt that the facilities have been utilised at the minimum level. The underutilised resources have become a waste and a liability for the community.

Estate Work

Thandikudi, Adalur, Panrimalai are the hills within a distance of 50 km from Sitharevu. Coffee estates are the major avenues for employment. About three hundred men and women are going daily to these hilly areas for employment. Earlier they used to go on foot. Now the estate owners are providing the transport expenses or provide vehicles to take them to the workspot. There is no organised union for the plantation workers. Average daily wage is Rs.20 to Rs.25 for women and Rs.30 to Rs.35 for men. Due to limited bus services, the crowd is thick during the morning and evening trip. People climb on to the roof of the buses. School going adolescent boys and girls are also going for estate employment during the weekend and other holidays.

Private Money Lenders

People's ignorance has been capitalised by many in the villages. Many money lenders come to the village and lend money at high rates of interest, namely 36 per cent, 48 per cent and it may go even up to 60 per cent. People who do not know the provisions available with the banks and the government have been under the influence of these money lenders. Some of the money lenders have earned several lakhs of rupees. They have their own system of lending. Varieties of loans have been floated in the society. Of them three are in practice in the village. They are daily repayment loan, weekly repayment loan and loan with mortgaging properties.

Daily Repayment : For a loan of Rs.100, the person who gets the loan will get Rs.85, after deducting Rs.15 as interest. He then has to repay one rupee daily for 100 days.

Weekly Repayment : For a loan of Rs.100, the person who gets the loan will get Rs.95 after deduction of Rs.5 as interest. Weekly repayment is at the rate of Rs.12.50 for 10 weeks.

Loan with Mortgage : At the rate of Rs.5 interest per month for Rs.100, after receiving materials like jewels, brass vessels as mortgage. About ten influential individuals are involved in this money lending business from the same village. Two parties from Madurai are also giving loan to the villagers. About three to five lakh rupees are in circulation in this private money lending.

Minor Forest Products

Honey, sikakai, amla, kadukai, kungilagam, bamboo, gum, kalpasam, herbal grass and fruits are being harvested from the forest and the hills and sold in the nearby towns. It provides employment opportunity for more than one hundred members everyday.

Local Library

It was established in the year 1965. There are about 5669 books in the library. On an average forty-one readers visit the library everyday. On an average nine books are being lent by the library to readers everyday. At present, there are about 611 members in the library. Youths are coming more in number and students are visiting during holidays. History, medicine, stories are the favourite subjects of the readers. It is functioning at the village common place. New construction will be started within two months. The village committee legally handed over the property to the local library authority.

Agriculture/Estate Products Trading Business

Pepper and coffee are the major products. These are purchased from the farmers and sold in the retail market at Dindigul, Madurai, Virudhunagar and Madras. The local traders learn about the market rate through newspapers. Those who have more money can procure more and earn more. A large number of traders are from the Muslim community. The cost of sorghum has gone up. It is used more for cattle feeding than for human consumption.

Farmer's Association

The Farmers Association was formed to safeguard the interests of the farming community. It was so popular among the farmers under the leadership of Narayanasamy Naidu. It was very active also. Now it is not so active and strong. The wetland farmers formed an association. Four measures of the native Marakkal of grains is given to the association which undertakes work like pond/tank maintenance, water management, channel maintenance and watch and ward assignment. The president is Mr. Nukulan Moopar.

Agriculture

Government schemes are not availed of by small and marginal farmers. Wages have been increased for the labourers as they demanded higher rate of wages comparing their position with others. New farmers are mostly from the Muslim community. Cash crops are preferred by farmers. Fifteen years back plantain was not cultivated. Now intensive cultivation of plantain, sugarcane, and cotton is practised. Drylands are now converted into orchards mango, guava, cashewnut, and sappota are cultivated. The farming expenses cannot be controlled. Wages are comparatively lower than in other area – Rs.45 to Rs.50 for men and Rs.25 to Rs.30 for women. The old practice of storing the products and selling whenever needed is not to be found now. They sell immediately. Seed stocking/process by farmers themselves is no longer in general practice. Most of work is being carried out on contract basis.

Dryland cultivation is being carried out by understanding and applying modern farm techniques like bunding, constructing check dam, and drip irrigation. Non-skilled labourers can get regular employment in agricultural sector. Vehicle availability/transport facility is helping the big farmers to transport their products to the market. Tools, equipment, machines and other implements are owned by farmers themselves for farming operations.

Loan assistance is needed for deepening well, and to dig well so as to make water available for irrigation. Earlier the labourer used to get agriculture commodities as wages. He also got other products like vegetables etc., from the land. Due to labour problem, the farmers are converting their land into groves of coconut, sugarcane, and banana. The labourers are not ready to cooperate with the farmers. Due to free electricity, well water irrigation is manageable.

October/November and March/April are considered off season for agricultural labourers. Drylands are converted into farming land.

Transportation facilities in the village

Two wheeler	-	40
Car	-	1
Jeep	-	1
Lorry	-	5
Tractor	-	7
Bicycle	-	40

Agriculture Allied Activities

To rear animals like cows, goats, sheep cowherd and shepherd are needed in the villages. But the practice of keeping a cowherd/ shepherd is no longer in vogue. Nobody is willing to do the function. Traditionally this work was assigned to two communities, namely Konar, popularly called Yadava and Mathari. Now it has become a business. Cattle farming is an entrepreneurial venture. People in the villages have given up the practice of rearing goat, sheep and cow. The milch animals give milk. Now they get milk from either the vendors or from the dairy farm. Grazing land is not available. The forest guards are not permitting the cattle to graze. Chemical fertiliser is widely used and easy to handle. Tractors are replacing cattle. The practice of sending children to school has been on the increase as a massive drive has been on. The fodder like sorghum is not available in plenty. The farmers are trying to engage in other types of economic activities and are not interested in cattle business. Free grazing of goats/sheep is strictly forbidden by private farmers. Broiler chicken business is taken up by three/four persons. New innovations/experiments in the agriculture allied field have not yet reached the villages. Concentrated feed cost is very high. Hence the poor cannot keep cattle. Three rich farmers are keeping about one thousand animals and gradually they are selling their cattle. The keeping of poultry is now limited. Wages of an agriculture labourer was Rs.18 to 20 in 1965 and in 1996 it has been increased to Rs.32 to 40. There is a coir factory which provides employment to twenty to thirty persons.

A Progressive Farmer

A progressive farmer is one who involves in all the work related to agriculture. He tries to avail of all the help and subsidies in the agriculture sector. He has a thorough knowledge of modern farming activities such as production, storage and sales.

Earlier the farmer used to get all the necessary food items and vegetables from the land. He used to do the necessary process and keep a portion for his consumption. Dhal, gram, grains, gingely oil, groundnut oil, were available all the time in their houses. Now-a-days they are selling everything after harvest. They are not keeping even the seed with them. They used to purchase seeds at the time of sowing from the merchant, by paying more money. They used to spend more time in their agricultural activities. Now even without visiting the field, their agricultural operation is completed on contract basis by labourers. The labourers are not sincere now. We cannot command them. In those days working hours were from dawn to dusk and now that pracitice has gone.

Perception of Youth of the Elders

In Tamil society, irrespective of the community, youth would respect the elders as the moral literature emphasises the importance of the elders in building up the family and community. This has been the practice. But now the trend has changed. Youth have no respect for elders. The culture of respecting the elders of the family and community has gone to the lowest ebb. Moreover the relationship between the youth and the elders of the family is primarily determined by the economic benefits transacted between the youth and the elders. As long as the youth are at the receiving end, they respect the elders. Now the trend has changed. The relationship between the youth and the elders is not so smooth either in the family or in the community. The strained relationship has been interpreted in many ways. It is perceived that the media have changed the perception of youth about life. Life comforts, and possessing dress material, electronic gadgets and leading western style of life constitute real and worthy life. People who have crossed sixty years of age have a perception that the hatred between the youth and the elders is due to the needs of the youth not being provided by the elders. Twenty to thirty years back both worked together and they had no time to think of things other than their work. In the villages father, mother, sons and daughters worked together in agriculture. A close intimate relationship between the youth and the elders was built up. But now the farmers have work only for three months. The rest of the year they while away the time in "chavadi" a public place where one can meet all kinds of people. When the youth are in the company of many away from the clutches of the parents they succumb to the pressures of the peer group. The life style portrayed by the parents of today's youth is not so attractive. So pleasure seeking is the main objective in life as portrayed by the media. The goods and articles produced and sold in the market are for stimulating the senses, consuming which will ultimately ruin the value system of the society.

How did individuals achieve progress?

In the whole transformation process individuals and families are becoming rich and prosperous over the years and some of them are becoming poor and poverty sticken. When they are asked to explain how certain families achieved prosperity they indicated a list of activities through which they achieved prosperity. They are given below in the form of a Table.

Sl.No.	*Community*	*Activities*
1.	Muslim	1. Going abroad 2. Purchasing land 3. Petty business 4. Commission trade 5. Mat weaving
2.	Moopanar	1. Agriculture 2. Encroachment of unreserved forest and dryland farming 3. Animal husbandry
3.	Servai	1. Agriculture 2. Coffee plantation (contract) 3. Brick kiln 4. Petty business (hotel, petty shop, tea stall)
4.	Pillai	1. Agriculture 2. Petty business
5.	Thevar	1. Agriculture/dryland farming 2. Petty shop/tea stall 3. Arrack distillation
6.	Harijan	1. Daily wage earning 2. Milch animal 3. Agriculture as labourers
7.	Asari & Naicker	1. Trade 2. Hotel

Vellalar Sangam

About 150 families belonging to Vellala community are living at

Sitharevu and they have formed a caste association. Each family contributes Rs.5 to the Sangam. They have a common land and they have a plan to build a building for common purposes.

They are giving scholarship to poor children belonging to the Pillai community. They have chairs for the Sangam and they are given for rent. Youths have a separate association in the name of V.O.C. The Sangam helps the members during celebrations in the member's family like marriage, death, puberty etc. both by contributing money and extending moral support.

Political Awareness

People understand the role and responsibilities of the State, Central and local government. They maintain that panchayati raj institutions have to provide basic facilities to the people. They know the value of reservation for women and SC/ST. They know about the gram sabha and its functions as they were in olden days. Their demand is for more power to local bodies. Youth are coming forward to contest in elections to all representative institutions. Power and money are playing a vital role in the elections.

The Central Government has got enormous powers. Decision making in local bodies is quick and responsive. They feel that autonomy is essential for the progress of the state as well as local bodies. Details of government schemes are not known to the public. They feel that good relationship between Centre and State is essential. The panchayat election was not fairly conducted. Party politics in village panchayat election is not harmful as the candidates are accountable to the party. Micro level plan can be carried out in the villages.

Families have been divided on party lines. Each individual enlists himself or herself in a party. It is a kind of business proposition for the individual. Individuals are earning facility or money. People are politically conscious and aware. At the dawn of Independence there was no such political consciousness. They just went to the booth and casted their votes.

Social Awareness

People have realised that one has to respect other communities. People are realising the importance of women's rights. Women have limitation in public activities. People feel that they have a right to criticise the government. Caste superiority/inferiority is now coming in to the open. SC youths are organised and attempt to challenge the other backward castes. Political parties organise awareness camps for women's equality. Gram sabha could not function successfully. People understand the importance of afforestation and plant tree saplings in their field. Government acts/schemes are protecting the SC community.

Muslim women do not come out and involve themselves in public affairs. The SC community does not get any recognition during the temple celebration. The SCs now know their rights and privileges. The BC women are not permitted to go out freely.

Peer group

Friendship flourishes among the youth of all caste groups for games, swimming, climbing trees, watching films. Youth now becoming addict to the habit of smoking and drinking alcohol. Classical music and stories were prime attractions of the people in those days. Now modern life style demands something different. Reading of Tamil magazines is a new trend among the modern youth. But the quality and nature of the magazines are always not development oriented.

Nyaya Panchayat

The system of Nyaya Panchayat is not as strong as in earlier days. Elders are not showing interest in this system as they are not respected by the youth. Politicians are dominating the whole social process. Individual differences become hurdle in delivering judgement. Rich persons do not readily accept the Nyaya Panchayat. They prefer to go to the police station. Those who are able to spend more can get favourable decisions. Apart from castewise panchayats there is a Common Panchayat in which the leaders sit in a common place and settle disputes. Only very petty issues are now dealt with. But, earlier, no case was referred to police.

A Muslim Jamat is also functioning and the committee members are elected. The issues handled by the Nyaya panchayat are: property dispute among brothers and between neighbours, women's issues, issues between castes, and problems in money transaction. Panchayat members can be encouraged to participate. The Jamat deals with divorce problems.

Nyaya Panchayat system in SC (Christian) community is also functioning and ten persons are selected based on their merit and honesty. They deal with land, house site, loan between persons, property and family disputes. Punishments are fine or prostration before the community seeking pardon. Exchange of betel leaf and areca nut and accepting watermark compromise. In the Moopanar community it is usual that there will be a large gathering when Nyaya Panchayat is convened. Political interference exists in all communities in the panchayat. Yet it is functioning. Political influence in Jamat meeting is much less compared to that in other communities. The number of panchayats are now reduced due to the behavioural changes among villagers. The panchayats will not intervene in the disputes of the political parties in the villages. People are drawn from educated, rich and political segments for Nyaya Panchayats. Due to political developments and economic transformation, the role of traditional community is not effective in many respects.

Scheduled Castes and Scheduled Tribes

Harijan youths learn new skills and migrate to cities for varied jobs. The key positions in political parties of local units are not held by SC. The differences between SC Hindu and SC Christian are now reduced in general. They avail themselves of popularly known schemes. A women's sangam is functioning with the help of an NGO from Devadanapatti. They have understood the importance of women's education. SC and ST accept food if they are served on leaf and not in coconut shells. They accept that there is considerable improvement in their level of education, dress and behaviour. They are shedding their inferiority feeling and slave attitude. Still they cannot contest in unreserved constituencies for positions. Calling others *ayya, swami* is considered 'not necessary'. The SC youth discourage their fathers from behaving like slaves. By migration to industrial cities like Thirupur and Coimbatore the youths are exposed to urban situations and they form Ambedkar Manram to articulate their problems. Able leaders are not available in SC community. Due to the influence of political parties, now the BC are mingling with the SC and their social functions. Instead of supporting one political party, now SCs are in almost all political parties. They are not contributing to the common fund. So the emergence of leadership from this community is very difficult. Even among SC those who are educated and developed are not mingling with other SCs. They don't have chance to learn skills other than agriculture.

Scheduled Castes Community Leadership

In the SC community the traditional leaders are called as 1. Nattanmai, 2. Servai and 3. Maniyakar

Nattanmai is the chief functionary; Servai is the secondary position and Maniyakar is the third position. These positions are hereditary in nature. It is said that, among the SC communities, families are grouped in kinship, named *pangalis*. The one who got the right over the temple administration is called Nattanmai. The pangalis of this nattanmai are eligible to be named Nattanmai, if replacement of the existing Nattanmai becomes necessary for any reason. Individuals from the other positions like servai or maniyakar are not eligible to become nattanmai by virtue of removal of standing nattanmai. Like this the position of servai and maniyakar also herditary, limited to *pangalis* only. The rest are the common citizens who are able to criticise and comment on the activities of the nattanmai. Others can demand replacement of the wrong doers and request to name some others to be positioned in the respective positions.

Nattanmai is the chief. He has to be informed about marriage and all other events in each family. He is the first person attending those events. The wife of the nattanmai traditionally holds the significant leadership during functions like puberty ceremony.

The Nattanmai's leadership quality will be tested during the temple celebrations as it consists of so many responsibilities like collection of donation, individual contribution, arrangements for pooja, pongal and other things and also he has to submit accounts for each and every item of expenditure at the common assembly, after the temple celebration. This traditional leadership is unique to SC community, whereas, among the SC Christians, the leaders are selected. Everybody is eligible to become leader.

Kitchen Practice

First there is a total transformation in using vessels in household activities. Mud pots were used by all in those days. The rich, apart from mud pots, had vessels of silver and other costly metals. Now, irrespective of the economic position, stainless steel household utensils are the rule. Apart from stainless steel, plastic has become a household name to supplement stainless steel. Ovens were made of bricks and sand. People used only fuelwood collected from the village. Now there is no facility in the village to collect fuelwoods. People used to grow a variety of plants in the kitchen gardens and they got a few vegetables from the kitchen gardens. Now, there is no such practice and everything has to be purchased from the market. People had an environmental sense and they grew plants and trees. Green cover was their dream. The concept of large scale constructions and building infrastructural facilities has damaged the perception of the people.

Child Care

Children were considered gifts of the divine in those days. Traditional methods were adopted to protect pregnant women. Herbal medicines were used for all diseases. People never went to hospitals for delivery. There was no such facility near the village.

Infant mortality was very high. But now the government has taken the initiative to provide facilities and introduce schemes to protect pregnant women. From conception to delivery of babies a variety of schemes have been introduced by the government. In the past, enough care was not taken to bringup the children.

Pilgrimages

Deeply devoted, religious minded and pious individuals made pilgrimages to various holy places in those days. But now people are not having such commitment and sense of devotion and yet they make pilgrimages. The number is increasing. Now pilgrimage teams have been formed in the rural areas and they follow the path of political parties in organising this programme.

The Problems They Face

* Community still has control over the individuals.
* Even within the community an individual is not able to select his or her partner.
* Equality between sexes is only on the lips in the rural areas.
* The government scheme for intercaste marriage is beneficial to urban people not to the rural poor.
* The expectation of the people has reached its zenith.

Problem of Labour

As monsoon never failed in those days. the employment opportunity was adequate and hence there was no problem for the poor in getting opportunity to work in the farm sector. But the wages for the poor were very low. For their work they were paid only in kind. But now there is no adequate employment opportunity for the poor in the rural areas. At present wages have been fixed in cash by the government.

Village Celebration

Varadaraja Perumal Temple

It is under the jurisdiction of the Hindu Religious and Charitable Endowment administration. Its history is that it was built during the time of Thirumalai Nayakar of Madurai. It is said that originally, the *pooja* was performed by the Naicker community. But for the past 250 years, it has done by the Ayyangar community. Two acres, 65 kuzhi dryland and 2 kuzhi wetland are endowed to the temple. The landed properties are not available now. The tenants are using them.

Celebration Season

1. Chithirai
2. Adi
3. Sri Rama Navami
4. Sri Vishnu Navami
5. Vijayadasami

Rs.10,000 has been collected through Hundi during the *Chithirai* festival. The following communities show concern for the temple and its affairs: Servai, Moopar, Pillai and Naicker. Now the government appointed trustees are helping in temple administration. Moopar now-a-days do not give much attention to this temple. They are renovating their community temple and improving its architectural construction. Only upper middle class people used to give *Archana* and come and worship during the marriage day. SC entry is not avoided. Even then they generally worship at the outside cella, though a few do come inside.

Load men

About 20 persons are working as load men at Sitharevu village. They are employed by the traders who mostly deal with the agricultural commodities like pepper, lemon, fruits (banana, jack), grains, paddy. They are helping in weighing and transporting, loading and unloading. They get contract wages at the rate of Rs.4 per bag. They transport by bicycle also. On an average they earn Rs.75 daily. The majority of the load men are Muslims. Efforts have been initiated to organise a union/sangam for them. But it has not materialised due to political differences.

Nutritional Awareness

Mutton stall	-	7
Broiler stall	-	2
Egg stall	-	1

Once the mutton stall owner had to wait till afternoon to complete his sale. Now before 8 A.M. the customers rush and complete the purchase. This practice shows their love for food. It has become a weekly affair. Taking egg is also routine.

Rural Business

Provision store	-	13
Petty shop	-	15
Hotel/Tea stall	-	14
Vegetable shop	-	13

Farmers themselves are directly involved in sales. The place once named "temple side" is now called *Bazaar of Sitharevu.*

Case Study (Caste Vs. Politics)

To provide house site to the Harijans, a site was proposed. This land belonged to a local Muslim. For about 80 houses, @ 3 cent each, about 2 acre land was identified and recommended to the government for acquisition. The land owner made a false claim that the site was a part of the grave yard of the Muslim community. He and other Muslims arranged a false document to show that it was a part of a graveyard. But the Tahsildar, visiting for inspection, rejected their claim and recommended acquisition. The case was taken to court and the court also delivered judgement favouring the cause of the Harijans.

At this juncture the general election came. The problem was referred to and the local DMK candidate assured to extend all his help to acquire the site for the colony. So all the SCs voted for the DMK. But, after the election, the issue was sidelined by saying that it was under judicial custody. Then the panchayat election was announced. The presidential candidate was a Muslim who promised to get the land. After his success, he too was not ready to help. Due to this the SC community decided to show its protest by joining hands with Moopanar community who were opposed to the Muslim President. They planned to start a branch of B.J.P. This may create tension in the village, as the Muslims and Hindus are so far maintained good relationship. BJP openly seems to be their opposition party. This is one of the dimensions with regard to caste versus politics, and religion versus politics at Sitharevu.

Moopanar-Mutharayar

Five types of roles are played by community leaders during temple celebration :

1. Account/administration
2. Procession —Deity lifting
3. Watchers —Guardians of temple and properties
4. Kodangi --drumabeaters
5. Poojari —the purohit

Each type has a number of families and a representative from them is allowed to perform the relevant role.

Preference is given to persons who are honest, knowledgeable and extroverted. These representatives are combined into a committee which is the supreme body executing all assigned work for the general welfare of the community.

Transformation takes place in the following areas

* Number of houses have increased.
* People opt for nuclear family.
* Entrepreneurship culture has not developed even though such opportunities are available.
* Parents are complacent with their wards completing primary level education.
* The income of the family has increased. Equally their needs have also increased.
* Those who understand the rational of income expenditure are conducting their life economically and they progress well.
* Moopanar community is considered the sons of soil and they are heirs of siddhar.
* The villagers now have better exposure, establish contact with the outside world and increase their understanding.
* Lethargy and slowness of the villagers have changed. Those who do not have work are whiling away their time.
* Thevar community is the pioneer in encouraging dowry items for their daughters in the areas of this study.
* Sitting at common places and whiling away the time is now reduced.
* Consuming liquor, purchasing lottery tickets, and watching films cinema are the major habits among the working classmen.
* People used to go to bed earlier and got up earlier in those days. Now due to cinema, video, cable TV programmes, villagers are not going to bed early.
* The cunningness and malpractices of traders, shop keepers are now restricted. People are aware about weight, quality, price of commodities and hence they have control over their affairs.
* Theft practices among villagers are now considered shameful for the individuals.
* The rich estate owners in Pattiveeranpatti are obstacles to any industrialization in the area due to the fear of labour scarcity for their plantation work.
* Still the burden of the family is on the women's shoulders. The earning of men is not fully utilised for the family. They spend

on their own interests and give only a part to the family.

* When youth are controlled by the elders in their family, they move away from the normal track of the family.
* Christian missionaries are doing a lot of service work which leads to conversion from Hinduism to Christianity.
* Saving habit has gone into oblivion.
* Habit of storing food material has gone and people purchase everyday.
* Families of Dhobi community now do not like to get meals/ eatables from others and they treat it as a insult to their self-respect.
* About 50 per cent used to give groundnut/gingely and get oil from native ghani.
* Practice of managing the common properties by the community has gone.
* Religious fanaticism has mounted in both religions, Hinduism and Islam.
* Usage of kerosene stove is increased in the village. Some have air-stove too as fuelwood is scarce in the rural areas now.
* Awareness of smokeless chulah has been generated among middle class people only.
* Even the poor are not using earthen pots. They have only aluminium, stainless steel and plastic materials/vessels.
* Ragi flour is available in packets. The traditional process of grinding is now avoided.
* Variety of greens were available in plenty in the field in those days.
* Bathroom facilities are available at home particularly in Muslim communities. Temporary arrangements are made in middle class families. The poor have some thatched sheds and use them as bathroom.
* Latrine is also more in use in the Muslim community. New buildings have latrine facilities (Among 3000 families, only 500 have latrine facilities).
* Taking tiffin in hotel has increased.
* Drinking of tea, coffee in hotel has increased.
* People are realising the importance of nutritious diet.

* Purchasing of more vegetables and fruits.
* Mutton stall number has increased (15 shops).
* Egg sale has increased.
* Earlier the villagers had a variety of dhal and gram and kept them for the whole year. Due to change of cropping pattern, now the availability of grams and dhals is limited. Even the agricultural families are purchasing from shops.
* Some farmers used to sell their paddy without keeping for their consumption. They are purchasing ration rice and use the same as it is cheap.
* Wheat is used by middle class people. The working class do not use wheat as it is not a tasty item. Rice, old or new is used for lunch.
* Children are demanding eatables from shops. The practice of preparing eatables like athirasam, murukku, porivilangai are not in practice even among the rich families. Everything is purchased from shops.
* Children do not like the food items prepared from sorghum, ragi and wheat. Mothers promptly get nutritious flour from the balwadi and utilise it for children or for themselves.
* Children earlier used to eat dryland products like a variety of beans.
* Dhal and vadai were the special items during the special days of feasting in to earlier period. Now it has become a common item, purchased everyday from hotel even by poor families.
* Native vegetables like pumpkin, beans, bitter gourd are now replaced by carrot, beetroot, cabbage etc.
* The practice of mixing raw rice with jaggery and coconut and eating in the evening as snacks is now not in practice.
* The flour of millets mixed with jaggery or prepared as roti was eaten as snacks in those days.
* Fish is available from Athoor dam and is purchased by the majority of the families.
* Drinking horlicks/bournvita in the evening or at night is in vogue in some of the middle class families.
* Major food items like grains, dhals, grams, tamarind, vegetables were more or less freely available in those days. Now everything

is purchased by villagers in the market only.

* Taking food in time is the new habit among the villagers.
* Hand pounded rice was a regular food in those days.
* Taking tiffin at home/hotel is now convener even among working community.
* The poor have tiffin during the festival day. But the working men take tiffin from hotel whenever they feel like it.
* Earlier villagers had the practice of eating sprouted grams.
* Political leaders now get importance during the marriage day.
* Villagers like to have some non-vegetarian item in their menu.
* Earlier, the workers/poor did not have cash in their hand. So they were not able to purchase rice. Now they are purchasing in shops as well as in the ration shop.
* Buttermilk/curd was available in every house earlier.
* Poor people used to get rice meal for their children from the rich.
* Children are eating several eatables like rice corn, toffees and biscuits.
* Drinking of old rice water everyday morning —a habit earlier, is now discontinued.
* The porridge of grain husk was prepared and given to children for nutrition.
* Children and even adults used to be attracted to tasting the dried sorghum corn for its unique taste in those days.

3

PEOPLE'S ENTITLEMENTS

The fiftieth year of Independence has come to a close, stock taking of success and failure has also been done and popularising the new policy options of the government in tune with the trend in the world, irrespective of the party in terms of economy and governance, has not totally changed the role and responsibilities of the State. To cope with the new requirement the State may make modifications in terms of its role and function but it does not mean that it evades the primary duties. It can move from the platform of a provider to that of a facilitator. At the same time it has to facilitate every individual to decide his destiny. In this context the core duty of the State remains unaltered and, especially in India, still the requirement of the State to equalise the communities in terms of opportunities is an imperative one.

To take stock of the situation about the role of the government from the perception of the citizen, villagers, both men and women, have been contacted and a wide range of questions have been asked and reactions have been recorded and observed. The central concern of the study is whether the State has performed its inextricably inescapable function of fulfilling the entitlements of the citizens. The State, whether it was in the formative years of nation-state building or in the globalised and liberalised economy or in the ensuing years of global governance, has certain unalterable responsibilities which cannot be lost sight of as long as the State stays to operate in the society as a mighty entity.

In this study the entitlements which have been assured to the people through various means from constitution to political parties have been ensured by the functioning of the state have to be examined. Specifically a cluster of villages have been selected keeping in mind that the villages have to reflect the reality in the sense that peculiarities have to be reflected. This study has two strong assumptions, namely that there is no dispute over the massive achievements of the state at the macro level and that equally, it has its own failures which have been the dark side of the state. The failure is in fulfilling the basic needs of the people that, too after fifty years of democratic governance. This area draws the attention of all. To what extent it has fulfilled and to what extent the State has to perform its role to fulfil the unfulfilled needs is the major focus of this work.

Mostly the poor segment in the villages have been approached in this regard. The data represent the poor segment and the village community. Their primary and essential needs have been concentrated while discussing them with the respondents. National security has been the concern of the State all along, but food security of the poor is much more important than national security. Though enough arrangements have been made to ensure supply of food, whether they reach the people or not is the question. The respondents who responded to the questions on their food position are mostly married middle aged, downtrodden, backward and SC community, agricultural labourers, small farmers, illiterate and sem-iliterate. The working class who constitute the major section in the village go for work to earn their livelihood. The majority go for daily cash wages and the minority go for kind wages. Yet they are not sure how long they will get employment. Employment opportunities created by the State through its schemes and the opportunity provided in the village by the farmers are not sufficient to manage their life. What they earn during six months has to be retained for another six months. One positive aspect is that whether they have power to purchase food material or not, food materials are available in the villages in the open market. But the price is very high. None have the capacity to store food material for at least a month. At the maximum they can store it for a week. Two things are assured to them. Somehow or other employment opportunity has been created either by nature through rain or by the government schemes but these opportunities are not for the whole year and they have never had that experience. Hence their physiological system has developed to the extent of taking food twice a day or once a day with a snack instead of a meal. When they get two meals a day in an assured manner, they will be the happiest creatures on earth. There is no such assurance. There is a system called Public Distribution System (PDS) which has been created to ensure their entitlements. Yet food materials to the required amount have not been provided to the people and at the price affordable for the people. Apart from this, it is not the availability of material but the capacity of the people to purchase the same to safeguard their interest. It is obvious that the State, by its policies, has not provided opportunities to earn their livelihood or at least secured their food. Yet people are managing their affairs through the institutions available at their end however bad or exploitative they are.

Pawnbrokers and local money lenders have provided assistance to the poor. They get loans from them and repay the loans when they earn money through their employment. From the point of view of others the system is exploitative, but, for the poor there is no other alternative excepting going to them for their help to run their life. People do not have the habit of saving. During the season they earn but do not save. Whatever they earn has to be utilised to repay the loan and to purchase consumables. People have the practice of mortgaging the utensils, gold ornaments and getting money and spending the same for securing food. Even if they get money, they are not in a position to purchase food material from the public distribution system. Every family should have a ration card and it is considered a citizenship card and, for all practical purposes the ration card is a reference card. But in the villages, many families have several ration cards while the poor, who have no access to influential persons, may not get a ration card. Of the persons interviewed, 73 said that they have no ration cards. They further said that they have been observing that some of the families have three cards or four cards. The public distribution system has to ensure food security at least for the poorest sector. Nearly 80 respondents said that they are not getting their entitlements from the ration shops as they are shared among the wealthy and influential families which have got political connections. Though 64 per cent of the respondents agreed that they are getting their provisions from the ration shop, they informed that what they are getting from the system is less in quantity and poor in quality and sometimes goods rejected in open market and then supplied through the Public Distribution System.

Next to the quantity of food and the system through which it is being supplied, quality of food and its nutritive value is important in the context of developing the human resources. First, people should have awareness about the quality of food. One has to take to maintain his/her health. In most of the villages people do not have the needed awareness about the quality of food. Children are not brought up in the manner in which they ought to be brought up by giving nutritious food. Though the government has introduced nutritious noon meal scheme for the school going children, the quality of the food is not ensured. Large scale pilferage and corruption takes place in this scheme. The concept of health is not so important from the perspective of the people.

Ensuring a living space legitimately for every citizen is the responsibility of the State. For the past fifty years schemes have proliferated both for providing space and to construct houses in the space provided. Yet problems are alive in the villages. Of the respondents, 24 per cent said that the patta has not been given to them. Some of them are living in *poramboke* land. They have no legitimate right unless it is legitimised through a document. Of the 225 respondents interviewed, 207 said that they have not received any financial assistance from any agency to build houses. In providing *patta* the State had performed its function well but, in providing financial assistance, it has not done its best for all irrespective of the community. For SC and ST there is a clear-cut scheme.

Yet another problem the people face in the rural areas is drinking water supply. First, it should be made available to all. Then it should be very near to the peoples settlement. While providing water supply, the water should be protected and hence it should be clean, for which facilities are available in the local bodies to provide hand pump, overhead tank and pipeline to all the settlements. In the villages hand pumps, overhead tanks, individual wells, community wells, community tanks are available. All are being used by the people. The government should not think that the responsibility of the government is over by merely providing water. Water quality is to be ensured. Nearly about 47 per cent of the respondents said that they are taking only hard water because there is no other alternative. Even though water points are available, water is not available throughout the year. People are not ensured adequate water supply to meet their requirements. Even after spending huge amount of money for providing drinking water supply they are not able to get safe water for the full year. Maintaining the safety of water is more important than providing water. It is very rare to find this phenomenon. Nobody knows in the village what should be done in the tank to purify the water. Chlorination has to be done periodically to ensure safe drinking water. There is no dearth of means but a lack of commitment on the part of the officials plays havoc with the health of the people.

Sanitation and drainage are the two important key elements which ensure the health and development of mankind and the society. When the concept of sanitation is taken up for discussion everyone in the educated circle would think of toilet. In the Indian context it cannot be so. It is not providing toilets alone. It is a culture by itself. Unless people have proper orientation on sanitation it is very difficult to maintain sanitation in the villages. There is obvious evidence in the villages that the public toilets provided by the Government are unutilised. In our country of variegated geography and location-specific issues of soil, uniform pattern of solution will not be of much use. Hence solutions will vary from region to region. In the rural areas both at the individual level and at the community level, conception of sanitation is very poor. But, in the urban areas, at the individual level, perfect sanitation is maintained and, at the community level, there is no such conception and people do not care about sanitation.

In the rural areas it is very difficult to provide toilet facility as we are providing now as it would consume a large quantity of water. In most of the dry areas it is very difficult to find water even for drinking purposes. Orientation to people about sanitation is more important than providing sanitary facilities. There is no second opinion about the role to be played by the State in providing the same. Nearly 90 per cent of the people stated that they are not aware of the implications of insanitation in the society. They further said that they have no facilities excepting the open ground meant for nature's call. Ten per cent of respondents said that they have toilet facilities in their houses.

People do not have any knowledge of the problem of sewage. Waste disposal is now a menace everywhere as the wastes are mixed and not in decomposable form. It is a massive programme the State has to organise, not with the workers employed by the government. It should be with the involvement of the people and with their direct and active participation. It seemed from their observation that there is no reaction among the people to the stagnation of waste water in front of every house. The stagnated waste water and the drainage flowing in front of every house are the places where all diseases are born.

Primary health centres and hospitals are the basic necessities of the people to maintain their health. It is the duty of the government to provide such facilities. Policies have been chalked out and accordingly facilities have been created. The problem here is the facilities are created but these facilities are not in a position to be utilised by the people and hence they have been denied the use of these facilities. Government-operated medical institutions have got a very poor name among the people. People have lost faith in the institutions managed by the government. People prefer to spend money for their health even though there are facilities that could be used free of cost. Neither the government nor the people who are all involved in running the institutions are sensitive towards this problem. People are also passive as facilities are available at cost. This is the alternative arrangement provided by the individuals. The failure of the State is considered an opportunity for the private individual to earn money. For the people it is service. Of the people questioned, 84 per cent felt that the facilities in the hospitals and primary health centres are inadequate and they cannot be used.

The right to live is a fundamental right and a fundamental duty of the government. Right to peaceful living should also be ensured. Supply of illicit liquor is a menace which threatens the life of many.

Most of the women pointed to the deplorable situation. The life of women in many of the families in which husbands are addicted to liquor is miserable. It cannot be changed immediately by advising them in the family. It requires strong, convinced and determined steps on the part of the government.

Education is yet another entitlement which has to be ensured to the people by the authorities of the State. Primarily schools have to be created and they should be equipped with modern facilities. Further the quality of education should also be ensured. From the discussions of the people it is inferred that schools are there, teachers are available, but with inadequate facilities. The quality of education provided in the public schools compelled the parents to put their wards in the private schools and thereby the government has enabled the private individuals to start educational institutions with profit motive. The respondents indicated that the facilities like classroom, teachers, toilets, drinking water supply, equipments, play ground are not adequate. Some of them argued that the public exchequer is being wasted in organising schools and appointing leaders in the rural areas but there is no assurance from the government of quality education.

The respondents, in an angry mood, reacted that there are three types of educational system in our province, namely education to the poor, education to the middle class and education to the rich. Even in education the poor are being exploited. The middle class and the rich are able to manage as they have got sufficient income but the poor have ambition to educate their wards but their economic condition is so poor that it will not allow them to put their wards in the schools providing quality education. The education which the poor receive will not enhance their capacity to reach higher positions. So the poor have to remain poor. Unless this defect is rectified, there is no scope for social justice in the rural areas. Hence the State has to take many initiatives to remove the maladies in the system.

Man or woman who has no assets to keep himself or herself to be employed and to earn their livelihood. They are wholly dependent on the mercy of nature and that too for only six months if nature helps fully by its downpour and otherwise their life is miserable.

The landless labourers are not only struggling for employment opportunity but also to get their due wages for their labour. Of the respondents, 88 per cent said that they got employment opportunity for a maximum of hundred days in a year while, 92 per cent of the respondents require of full employment opportunity for the whole year to realise their objectives and dreams. For want of employment opportunity, they have to migrate from their village and settle in some other areas where employment opportunities are available. In the course of migration, their children's education is being disturbed. Sometimes they also join their parents. The sufferings are acute in some families.

Clothing is yet another necessity which has to be ensured. Normally the poor do not have the ambition of storing dresses beyond the basic requirement as their economy will not permit them to do so. Of the respondents, 43 per cent said that they have no adequate clothes and hence they have been in desperate need of clothes from the government. They appreciated the scheme of distributing *saris* and *dothis* to the poor every year free of cost. They further explained that, however, this scheme is ill conceived: it has not really benefited the poorest strata. If the scheme is perfectly executed the beneficiaries would get quality articles from the government and the dress material will have durability.

Roads and transport are essential factors for development. In Tamil Nadu both roads and transport are in tune with the requirements of the people. Even small hamlets have these facilities. Mini bus service has also been introduced to reach the remote villages. But the problem lies in the bus fare. Transport vehicles are carrying goods from the villages to cities and from the cities to the villages. For the rich and the middle class it is not a problem, but for the poor it takes away a sizeable portion of their earnings.

Thus the entitlements are not ensured fully to the rural poor. On some of the facilities steps have been taken earnestly by the government authorities yet they have not been fully ensured. Some of the facilities have been provided but they are not maintained properly to deliver the goods to the people. Even if there are differences among the collectivities, if the basic needs are met by the intervention of the government through its institutional mechanism, people in the villages would lead a peaceful life, which needs the immediate attention of the government.

4

RESEARCHER'S OBSERVATION

Apart from being an individual born and brought up in a rural atmosphere, I have been keenly and curiously watching the activities of the people in the rural areas, their behaviour, belief system and attitude towards life for the past ten years. I am part of the culture of the rural areas and, yet, I feel understanding the people and their behaviour is not so easy. Their views, belief system, values and attitudes towards life are complex in nature and are beyond comprehension through the established theories of Sociology, Anthropology and Psychology.

It is easy to observe the changes that have taken place in physical infrastructural facilities such as institutions, communication system, material that are provided and used in day to day life, economic activities, political activities and cultural activities. It is very difficult to understand the thought process of the people who live in the rural areas. It is a highly difficult job to make a pattern out of the behaviour of the people and its linkages with their thought process.

While interacting with elders in the villages one would get an enormous quantity of information about the science, the technology, the medicine and the way of life practised over the years. To weave the information into a pattern of behaviour and principles one requires great acumen. I was astonished when a villager explained the methods of climate management in those days by the farmers of the villages. In the absence of meteorological stations, people relied on certain principles carefully observed in the society with the help of a few culturally literate intellectuals who had a record of history in folk songs. Thus farmers carried out their activities only with the help of a group which used to observe the behaviour of the moon and the sun and predict the climate more accurately than our meteorological stations. All farm practices were followed meticulously as per the direction of a group which guided the farmers based on their prediction.

There is yet another shocking discussion I had with a villager who had a profound knowledge about the fiscal economics of the villages. It is a stage where everybody talks about the devolution of financial powers from the central government to the state government and from state government to local governments. An old man in a village projected statistics by which a gram panchayat can give money to the state and the central government by making use of the natural resources. It is not a mere vision. He anchored his argument on the resources available in a village Karaikkeni in Madurai District, which happened to be his native place. At the dawn of Independence they had a reserve of two lakhs as savings since most of the natural resources were with the community and not with the government.

Yet another striking feature I found in a village was the country medicine. An uneducated woman was able to prepare medicine from just the herbs available in the nearby areas. She explained more than sixty items of medicine for different kinds of diseases and, for each and every item, she has strict instructions on how to prepare the medicine. The only drawback was that they were not patterned and the procedures had not been formulated as principles. If they are well researched, those medicines will provide enough scope for establishing a variety of industries to prepare medicines. She quoted many villages known for this herbal medicine, and in all those villages, a street was known as "Medical Practitioners' Street"—Vaidhyar Salai. In fact I started believing this practice only after recollecting the practices we had in my family. Till I attained the age of twenty I had no knowledge that I was taken to a hospital by my parents for my physical ailments. My mother was an undereducated woman who had sound knowledge of medicine. She has knowledge of the anatomy of the human body. She remembers everything in songs. Whether it is medicine or ailment or cultural festival she used to recollect points only from the songs. It is unfortunate that they are not recorded and properly researched.

There is yet another feature—the establishment of livelihood security in the villages among the people of the community. Agriculture was once the centre of activity, for which a variety of ancillary activities had to be carried out by making use of the skills of the people. On an average, seventeen skills were identified in the villages and all the skills provided an opportunity for work. Hence every individual was somehow involved in activity in one form or another. The energy of the people was properly utilised and channelised. Their activities had a direct link with nature. The relationship between nature and the human being was harmonious. One striking event I observed in village life in my native place was that I never saw an event of felling a tree unless it withered or fell due to natural calamity. I enquired of this feature with my parents when they refused to provide timber from my plantation to construct a house in a city where I started my career. My parents informed me that people plant saplings and nature provides firewood and needed timber to the needy and people should not disturb nature. The poor used to collect firewood, not by cutting saplings and small trees from the common property resources but from the trees withered naturally.

Moreover people had established a rapport with the plants by worshipping them. Each and every village had at least seven or eight places earmarked for worship, wherein neem trees were identified as the idol for worship. Such trees have sometimes crossed centuries. Today people mock at the community which performs pooja and ceremony to these trees by following the tradition. Yet, for many, they are values. People refuse to spend money for health and education but they spend money for conducting annual function and ceremony to the family Gods and community Gods, which, in appearance may be irrational, but, to the people, they are meaningful and they give solace to their heart and moreover they are the values which cannot be separated from them. Once *sun worship* was practised in the villages by the elders. Even in temples this worship pattern was recognised. Deities were installed. Festivals were celebrated regularly on an annual basis. There was a belief that those who practised sun worship will not get eye defects or ailments. This was caricatured once and it was considered irrational. But now professors from American Universities have conducted research into this issue of sun worship and brought out several volumes on the dimensions and implications of sun worship. Further sun worship has taken another dimension of *Yoga* called *sun yoga* and not worship. In tradition what we find are only premises and principles, not explanations. As we lack the methodology, we can not understand and explain these principles and premises.

For administration the nation-state administrative system has established administrative units for the convenience of the rulers and the bureaucracy. People had established several units for living, based on the guilds, comity of caste collectivities and topography. Their arrangements were natural in character as nations. Local community organisations were so powerful and established bondage among the individuals and families. No other organisation could match the local community organisations. Community organisations are evolved, and functional in nature. People have their own share in the organisation and their participation is voluntary. Moreover, they cherish values in it as they conduct temple festivals. Whether it be an organisation or institution or any activity, if they are considered by the people as their own, they will give their life to them as if they are saving their life.

Yet another unit was the family, which has a broader connotation to the people differing from the definition of the academics and researchers. Their definition was an inclusive one. It was not only a group including father, mother, grandfather, grandmother, sons and daughters. It stretched beyond and it included aunt, uncle and their sons and daughters. By following the key principles of the family system undivided properties for certain families over three generations are still in practice. Now we call dwelling units as families. For the people it is only a nomenclature. For instance, in a village, there are about twenty families and each family has its own name. "Chinnathamvedu" is a family, "Pullakuttivedu" is another family and, likewise, a village has twenty or thirty families. Each family has thirty or forty dwelling units. Now each and every dwelling unit is divided into several living units. Each family has a range of forty to two hundred members. The decisions are taken only after consultation with the head of the dwelling units. Whether poverty or prosperity, the family members share it. They have rigid norms.

Family has certain common properties. Yields from the common properties will have to be shared among the dwelling units. Somebody will be the head of the family and it is hereditary in character. He may be rich or poor. Irrespective of the economic status, head of the family will be respected by all. Head of the family is seen as the symbol of the values of the family. This institution was so powerful for several centuries. But we could not see the family today in the villages and we could see the traces of the families in the form of names, common properties and temple festivals. It is interesting to note that the government has given a definition to the concept of family. Family is always identified with door numbers. It is only a living space or unit. Family cards are given for the living units. Absolutely there is no correlation between the definition of the government and that of the community. State intervention has gone deep, even into the family. Thus functional units have been disturbed by the intervention of the government. While analysing the changes in the society through history one would find the influence of colonial administration both in thought and action.

One traditional institution which is so popular still is the temple. Temples are of different varieties. The State has established its own authority over them. People never like interference of external authority with their properties. Hence, when the community properties are taken over by the State through the Departments, families have joined together and established temples at local levels. They conduct festivals on their own. They mobilise resources through cash and kind and every individual dwelling unit has to contribute to the common programmes in the temples. Even the poorest dwelling units will also contribute liberally to the temple festivals. Families have their own roles and responsibilities. In the conduct of festivals, caste has its own role and they are functional in nature. Every caste has its own role to be performed in the temple. The whole system of the temple management rests with a committee approved by the heads of families in a village. Gradually more number of family deities and temples have been established to overcome the problems faced due to the caste hierarchy. One would find a plethora of temples and family Gods in each and every village.

Caste and other distinctions were felt by the individuals only when the State system began to distribute benefits to different collectivities. People were made to be conscious about their caste and religion only to get benefits and establish control over the resources. Gradually, in the process of expansion of State activities through building institutions by taking away the responsibilities of the families, individuals began to organise themselves as collectivities to bargain with the government and they have used the identity of caste and religion as the identities are attached to cherished values. Caste is a social entity which has a social role in a society as perceived by the people. But now it is a political entity which has a political role to be performed as people were made to perceive the distinct role of the caste and the religion.

Yet another feature of the people of the rural areas in terms of their behaviour is unique and striking. The way in which he or she treats other religions is unique. It has been caricatured many times by the intellectuals. People used to celebrate local temple festivals and apart from this, they made pilgrimages cutting across region and religion. Personally I have been seeing people, mostly Hindus, going to Vellankanni to offer their prayer to the church in the mode of Christians and while returning from the church, they used to go to Nagore to offer prayer in the famous mosque. After performing their prayer in the two holy places, they used to go to Sikkal temple (Lord Muruga) for worship. In one trip they used to visit all the three shrines. Where is fundamentalism? Where is parochialism? Where is secularism? Common men in the rural areas are always secular and broader in their approach. To them religion is personal. It should not be misused. But, at present, people are made to believe that these are identities which will fetch economic benefits and hence people have been driven to making use of the caste and religion.

"Whether Rama rules or Ravana rules, we don't bother" was a popular slogan among the people once. If one carefully analyses the proverb one would understand the deep meaning and underpinnings of the proverb. People, in their community life, had onerous responsibilities and they found time only to discharge their responsibilities. They did not mind who was ruling them, because they felt that their livelihood was being determined only by their activities. The modern government and its institutions are so complicated to them. Life has become so complicated in the modern world. To the people in the rural areas there is no difference between the colonial administration and the administration of the representative form of government. Exploitation, marginalization, corruption, domination of one group over another, and nepotism have been prevalent in both administrations.

Government institutions have created many roles and, to perform those roles, individuals have been recruited, by which people's responsibilities have been taken over by the government. The livelihood security was the affair of the community once but now it is in the hands of the government. Government is far away from the people. People do not have enough orientation to establish hold over the government and thereby the supremacy of the government is established.

Education is an important factor for development as perceived by all. But the meaning of the concept differs from the perspective of the so-called educated. Education means, in the formal sense, ability to speak, write and read and enhance the capacity of the individuals to tune into change. Particularly education refers to the increase in the capacity of the people in terms of productivity. In the villages, according to the statistics of the government, the majority of the people are uneducated. But, in terms of their wisdom, all are educated culturally. Despite all pull and pressure in politics, for the past fifty years, it is the culturally literate mass that has saved the country and the democracy from disaster. People know their land, soil, water, plants, topography, seasons, climate, animals, culture, and values without going into any formal system of education. People were once well versed about their relationship with nature. But now, to understand all those aspects, one has to go up to college. Simply because of the fact that society is regarded from the perspective of western education, one will say that the majority of the people are uneducated. By shifting the perspective of looking at the people from wisdom, Indian masses have a profound wisdom and knowledge and they have got the values for guiding the whole world. It is unfortunate that our approach has always been from the perspective of the materialistic west. This has marred the vision and the reality.

Yet another aspect which needs serious attention is maintenance and management of facilities provided to the communities. Roads, tanks, and other common properties had been maintained by the communities with the voluntary contribution of the members of the society. Because people felt that those are the properties of the community and moreover those properties had been yielding benefits to the poor and the rich simultaneously. They are the life line of the people. In the course of building the nation and the state people were driven away from the common property resources and they were taken away by the government. The process of taking away the properties of the communities started during the period of the British. The British had established the foundation for the modern governmental system in India by relegating the people to the background. People's organisations were totally disturbed. Now the government institutions have established and provided many facilities to the people and yet they are not properly maintained and managed either by the people or by the government. In the name of facilities and infrastructure natural order and ecosystem of the villages have been spoiled. After establishing communication facilities, all natural resources which are the properties of the people have been exploited. In the name of the state and government natural resources have been exploited for the advantage of the rich. Resources which had been preserved, protected by the community for centuries, have been totally exploited for producing materials and articles for sale by the rich with the support of the government. Hence natural resources have lost their lustre and their potential to contribute to the livelihood security of the poor and, thereby, the poor have lost their employment opportunity and started moving from rural areas to urban centres for gainful employment.

Political institutions are perceived as pivotal to the development of the society according to the so-called formally literate citizens. For the common men who lead a hand to mouth existence, their work is more important than any other things. They look at politicians with utmost respect in the belief that they work for the nation and, that is why, without expecting anything from the politicians they have been going to the booth and casting their votes continuously since Independence. They respect bureaucracy in the hope that our officials will do good things even though our officials are corrupt to the core. Here one important aspect has to be considered carefully. People have faith, hope and trust in politicians and officials, but the politicians and officials have no hope and faith in the people. The colonial mind-set still prevails among the politicians and the officials. Politicians and bureaucrats are corrupt to the core and they have no respect for the people. People are respected only during the time of election. After the election, people are not considered as citizens but as subjects, as if people are receivers and politicians are givers and officials are contributors. Millions and million of the masses never expect anything from the government. Intellectuals comment that they are fatalistic masses believing in fatalism. In reality they are not fatalistic in nature. They perceive that development of individual or family or collectivity depends fully on them rather than on the government, that government can act only as a facilitator, and, that people are the prime agents of development.

At the grassroots level many institutions have been established by the government. But they are not successful and popular among the people. The New Panchayati Raj System has been established by the government through legislation and leaders have been elected by the people politically. New leadership has emerged in the rural areas yet the new leaders of the panchayats are not permitted to head the community as the people value very much the traditional leadership. For all the functions of the families and communities, traditional leaders called "Nattanmai" has to preside over and not the leader of the panchayat. The newly elected leaders in the panchayat institutions have well established connections with the government and political parties and yet they cannot be rated on par with traditional leaders as per the perception of the people in the villages.

Among the people there are two types of perceptions about development. For the old, values are more important, traditions are to be preserved. For the youth, economic development and social status are more important. Youth sincerely believe that the social status could be increased by enhancing their economic status or by acquiring wealth and materials. Elders sincerely believe that upholding values and traditions will alone save their family and community. Status of the family and community depends on the maintenance of values in the society as per the perception of the elders.

The increasing economic activities, acquiring more material wealth, adopting modern style of living, and increasing infrastructural facilities have not reduced the social tension and conflict among the individuals in the family, among the families in the community and among the communities in the society. Greater opportunity for economic development paves way for intense competition and conflict among the individuals, families and communities. Youth have been oriented in the process of conflict to achieve development which is contradictory to the ethos of the elders who maintain that peace, harmony and coexistence constitute development.

Transformations are wrought only in the outward appearance of the people. Inwardly they are traditional in nature. They are modern in appearance and traditional in thought. Transformations are not evolved over the years and they are brought about by the wilful and conscious efforts of the government. Government, by speeding up activities, accelerated the functioning of the collectivities to bring about material prosperity. Government initiated and accelerated human activities have not brought about sustainable development. There is a gap between the thought process of the government and the communities in the rural areas. It seems that the concepts of modernization, industrialization and westernization have completely suppressed the indigenous knowledge in science, technology, management and governance and, as a result, our credentials have not been exhibited to show the world that India has substantial amount of knowledge to achieve sustainable development with equity and values.

5

RURAL LIFE IN THE NEXT MILLENNIUM

The post cold war era has brought about a tumultuous change in all aspects of human life which makes the academics ponder over the very direction of the movement of humanity. Of late certain concepts, such as globalization, liberalization and structural adjustments, have been repeatedly trumped up, and have been drawing the attention of many people in the world. A spate of discussions are on both in favour of and against these concepts and yet the process has been initiated as it is a historical process which cannot be annulled by arguments and protests however valid and sound they are in the domain of knowledge. What is going on is the reality. The disappearance of bipolar world unleashed unlimited energy into the productive sectors which, in turn, opened humanity's eye to the opportunities in the world for prosperity. The fast moving humanity identified the barriers and obstacles in the process of their activities in order to achieve growth and development. Steps have been taken to remove all those irritants, ultimately resulting in globalization, liberalization and structural adjustment.

Human collectivities are not just like orderly and rhythmic entities moving in the direction shown to them. They are full of variations, imbalances, contradictions, incongruities and ambivalence in pursuing their interests through different means. The variations are due to the perception and the capacity of the individuals and collectivities. The communication revolution which has overtaken the society has stimulated the people to think and develop aspirations. The ever rising aspirations among the people have made the human collectivities identify the ways and means to realize their objectives. In the process of identifying the means to achieve their goals and realise their aspirations, conflicting perceptions, ideas and strategies emerge which blur the vision of the common man upon the process of development. Yet there is a dominating thought drawing the attention of humanity for its onward march. What is the key element dominating in the thought process of the humanity today to achieve progress and sustainability of the progress? It is the removal of restrictions, barriers and obstacles to make use of the material resources and potential powers of the humanity.

The global unrestrictedness in establishing contact with other societies in the world has to bring about togetherness to shape and share prosperity for the advantage of all in humanity. Marginalization, discrimination, segregation and alienation should not form part of the human collectivities. Equity and justice should attend the onward march of the humanity towards achieving prosperity. What we see at present in the unipolar world is not peaceful and equitable life situation but, instead, more gaps between the rich and the poor, more cases of alienating collectivities, and more number of groups being marginalised as the achieved prosperity does not percolate into the society as expected by the society. Hence societies are witnessing frequent social conflicts and sectarian wars. The real question then is, whom is this globalization or liberalization aimed at? Is it understandable to all? Is it advantageous to all? Basically it is a commodity oriented, growth centred and profit based activity. Flow of money, technological advancement, capacity building, changing the nature of the institutions to suit the new need and requirement are imperatives. But the question is whether all these activities will bring livelihood security to all the people in the world, maintain equity among collectivities, ensure environmental protection, and administer social justice and gender equity?

The new agenda enunciated through globalization of economy, liberalization and structural adjustment has its own conditions and yet they are not operationalised as they are conceived due to various constraints in the environments of the societies. Though it seems that the world is unipolar in practice it is not really unipolar but for all practical purposes, it is multipolar. Hence conditions for liberalized economic activities have not been created throughout the world uniformly through a centralized and institutionalized mechanism as human collectivities exert pressure on the government. The expected US hegemonic control over the nations of the world is not in vogue. Globalization, liberalization and structural adjustment mean many things to the perceivers as the perceptions of the leaders of the world are severely conditioned by the socio-political environment of their countries. Hence they take many forms and conditions for the above process which have been relaxed for the advantage of the nations mutually, while maintaining the relationship between nations and nations. Thus agreements and disagreements among the nations over the issue of operationalising the framework of globalization, liberalization and structural adjustment persist.

Selectivity is being practised among nations in operationalising the basic elements of globalization and liberalization. As expected, after the end of the cold war, development initiatives have not been smoothly allowed in all the countries without much resistance. Resistance was much stronger during the cold war period. All resistance from all quarters over this new economic venture emanates from the fundamental apprehension whether the new framework has got any resilience of human face. Thus the whole issue of the new initiative boils down to the basic issue of understanding and comprehending the new initiatives and evolving suitable operational devices in the respective social, economic and political environmental settings.

The polity of the developing countries, with the age old structure in the governing process, has not evolved resilient instruments to meet the challenges of the society. The democracy which they have practised cannot sustain for a long period as they fail to meet the increasing aspirations of the people. Yet another problem to be tackled by the state is the growing expectations and aspirations of the people due to the influence of the mass media. These two problems are to be visualized globally as the next millennium approaches. In most of the countries the perception gap between the governing elite (ruling elite) and the masses over the new initiatives has caused severe damage to the transformation process of their economy and society.

The problems we face on every front are due to the unrealised aspirations, excessively exploited resources, unutilised opportunities, unintegrated, and non-transformed energy of the people. In the past five development decades, humanity has witnessed a remarkable change through the accelerated activities to achieve prosperity and thereby created a great division between the rich and the poor. The process of sharing prosperity has created social conflict among the groups. A few societies and nations have achieved prosperity within a short span of time. Many of the nations are struggling to equip themselves to compete with others. How are the societies competing with each other to achieve prosperity? Competitions and their outcome are the results of the enhanced, transformed and integrated energies of the collectivities.

The government has acted in accordance with the aspirations of the people to make prosperity and given proper shape to the energy flow through policy options. The rest of the societies, through their state, tried to perceive and understand the process of development of the developed societies and tried to adopt the strategies of the developed societies to the developing societies also. But the collectivities of the developing societies do not have the requisite capacity and energy to cope with the new demand which is on a higher plane. Only a few groups are equipped with the requisite capacity to meet the challenges of the world. Hence there is a wide gap between the development model adopted in the developed societies and the status of the people in the developing societies who aspire to bring about development on par with the developed societies in terms of the energy level and its utility.

In the whole process of development, unexploited resources and available opportunities are made known to all and yet, to make use of these opportunities, the societies have to enhance their capacity. The impact of the developed societies has percolated into society very deeply and thereby the aspirations and expectations of the people have increased in an unprecedented manner. Even though the energy of the people is very low in the developing countries, their aspirations are very high. Thus the struggle in the society is to satisfy the unmet aspirations and expectations of the people.

In the developing countries, since the state has assumed absolute powers over the society, people have given their sovereignity to the state by abdicating their responsibilities. Thus all responsibilities are with the state and not with the people. Therefore, irrespective of the level of their capacity, people have developed aspirations and feel that the aspirations are their entitlements and such entitlements have to be realised by the intervention of the state. While the developing societies are confronting the consequences of statism and empowerment of the people to make them more responsible as participants of the development process, the developed societies have gone further in the development process.

The developed societies are trying to move further in the development process at a higher speed by enhancing the capacity of the people. To exploit the available resources and opportunities, the energy level of the people has to be enhanced. Enhancing the energy level of the people is a stupendous task. Development process of the society is not so smooth. So far the experience of the societies demonstrates that the institutional mechanism available within the society and the world has not uniformly adopted the norms to achieve development and equity. From micro to macro level there has been a tendency of exploiting the opportunity rather than doing justice by which distinctions and divisions are maintained.

Of course there are some initiatives at the global level to achieve sustainable development and equity among the collectivities throughout the world. But the suggestions and recommendations of the initiatives have not been successfully and effectively implemented in all the societies through the institutional mechanism legitimately evolved for governance, whereas all suggestions to achieve prosperity have been carried out through the same institutions, because these institutions are in the hands of the political and economic elite of the society. Equity is being thought of only when there is any problem disturbing the equilibrium of the political system. It has been demonstrated in the world that the achieved prosperity has not been shared with the community to meet the livelihood security of the poor and the marginalised, either through voluntarism or through initiatives of the state. Hence the existing belief system, that prosperity is meant for the wise who manage the political and economic system for their advantage, is going to be strengthened. Prosperity achieved in the societies has not solved the basic problems of the people in many countries. At the same time, the process of development of the groups and societies has demonstrated various success models for adoption.

Select individuals, groups and societies have adopted the models for prosperity and achieved the same and yet their prosperity has not transformed the life of the rest of the groups and societies. In all the five development decades competition to achieve prosperity has been intensive and escalated. The competition has resulted in raising the level of expectations and aspirations of the people. The whole state mechanism has been geared up to provide conducive conditions to have such competition and to succeed in the competition to earn more profit for the individuals and groups which can help the state to provide needed infrastructure to the marginalised and the alienated with the objective of keeping them in good living conditions without disturbing the stability of the system. Thus, in most of the societies, the state is a charity house doing the trusteeship work. It does not mean that development opportunities are not open to all.

Opportunities are always open, but, to participate in the development process as participants and partners, people should have the requisite energy and capacity. It is obvious from the experience of the society in the past that only a few societies have provided such opportunity to the people through the state to keep the energy at a high enough level to participate in the development process as partners of development. Many of the societies are struggling to keep the energy of the society to maintain the basic minimum for subsistence of the people. Thus a perceptible unbridged gap exists between and among the collectivities and societies in terms of the energy and skill. The escalating speed of the select groups and societies have pushed them up and above and far away from the rest of the groups and societies. The ever-widening gap between and among collectivities and societies has caused concern to the state.

The state, which is struggling to overcome the crisis, needs the assistance of the corporate sector to perform certain responsibilities along with NGOs, by which the structure of the governing institutions could be reduced sizably. While thinking of the new arrangements such as globalization and liberalization of economy and structural adjustment, steps and measures are always oriented to the flow of capital, materials and technology and not towards the problems of the humanity. That is why there are arguments that the human face is missing in the new reform measures. Yet another problem that humanity faces today is the competing role of the market and state over governing the society. The increased size and power of the state has not regulated the market and the society for the advantage of human collectivities. Neither the state nor the market has solved the basic problems of the society. Then one has to think of an appropriate institutional mechanism to regulate both the market and the state as they are in the clutches of the corporate sector. This does not mean both the sectors are to be undermined.

The new institutional mechanism would include micro level organizations of the people and macro level organizations of the nation-states to strengthen people's organizations in order to manage their affairs, achieve prosperity and distribute the benefits equitably to all segments of the society. The management of the state and the market is under the influence of the people's movement through their participation. The affluence of the market and the state have not been distributed to the poor to meet their basic needs as the poor are driven out from the process of development. Hence the need of the hour is to identify a humane governance through an alternative approach to development.

While looking at development one has to consider two aspects, namely the humanity and nature (man and his environment). Human groups' basic values, ethos and moorings, based on their cultural settings have to be preserved to make them remain integrated with the whole of humanity. Likewise, while making use of the resources from nature, one has to look at the resources from the perspective of the entitlement of the humanity and the future generations. The actions of the human collectivities while utilizing the natural resources should not disturb the balance and order of the cosmic system. To perform the above mentioned task, an appropriate institution could be found only at the micro level.

Local bodies are the vibrant institutions which have to be under the control of the people and, in turn, the local body institutions must act as institutions of the people and not the state. Over the years it has been proved beyond doubt that the commons, especially the natural resources, have been effectively protected and controlled by people's organizations. Equally the cultural ethos and moral values have been preserved by the local micro level institutions. The revolution in rising expectations among the people and the accelerated speed of the development process have made the human collectivities violate any norm or value, rule or procedure in the established system. In the process what we find in governance is corruption.

The mechanized process in administration and proliferated institutions for governance have made the government the sole authority for development and this has given the impression that the government has got overwhelming power to control humanity. The weight of the government on the people is very heavy and people do not have the resilience to bear the weight of the government. It is felt that it is high time to reduce the weight of the government. The experience of the past four decades has demonstrated that, by taking up more responsibilities of the people, the government (State) can successfully keep the people away from governance and hence a perpetual gap will be maintained. By sustaining the gap, people have forgotten their responsibilities as citizens to perform certain functions. The deliberate keeping away of the masses from the governing process has enabled the privileged class to make use of the resources and institutions without any interference from the society to make profit.

The governing institutional mechanism has been tuned in such a fashion as to work under the yoke of the market forces. Irresponsibilities have crept into the system as people are made irresponsible. The disturbance in the environment has cautioned the ruling (governing) elite to think of the long range implications of the degradation of environmental conditions. Likewise, the masses, who drifted away from the governing process, have acted in an irresponsible way by turning their emotions on culture, language and religion, which ultimately divided the human collectivities into many segments to work against each other, ultimately leading to the eruption of war among groups within nation and within religion. Thus the human energy which is to be used for higher level activities has been used to fight against each other.

Ethnic strife and sectarian wars in the world amply demonstrate that the human energy is being misused and wasted. Governing institutions, which are to concentrate much time on development and distribution, have been concentrating on crisis management. The repeated involvement of the government in crisis management has evolved and proliferated a large number of procedures to regulate humanity which, in turn, has made society loose its human face. The paradoxical situation of reducing military expenditure at the global level after the cold war and increasing government expenditure in maintaining law and order by multiplying the police institutions indicates the fact that war among nations has been reduced but conflict among groups has increased, for which the affluent market and total state are responsible.

To tackle the problems facing humanity, attempts have been made for several years at global level, even from the UN to the recently held World Social Summit but the outcome of all these efforts has not substantially altered the situation even though these efforts have disturbed the mind-set of the people who are at the helm of affairs. At the same time, market and state forces are very active and powerful and continue to do the functions by which many groups have been made to alienate themselves contrary to the expectations of the state and the market. It is also true that the concerted efforts of many to regulate both the state and the market have not yielded any substantial result. Further the market forces in this new era have taken a new course of action.

The framework which has been evolved among the partners of the market has not been sincerely adhered to and, as a result, market forces are also at conflict. Likewise the forces of the state are also at conflict. Never in the history of the world, has conflict brought about prosperity. Cooperation alone will bring about prosperity. Human energy is similar to the energy of the atom. Unmanaged energy of the human being is always a problem. When it is properly managed and regulated, human energy will produce the desired outcome to enhance the quality of life. To perfect and to enhance the human energy, micro level institutions are imperative.

The micro level institutions should be participatory in nature and flexible in action. They should be pro nature and pro-culture. These institutions should devolve powers and responsibilities to the people's organizations. People should find work to channelise their energy continuously. The ongoing transformation in the world provides enormous opportunities for work and the isolated activities at micro level could be integrated at macro level. Barriers have been removed for unification and integration. Unless the capacity of the people at different levels is enhanced, exploitation will be all the more pervasive in the world. Because of the fast changes in science and technology, the capacity of the people has to be enhanced and the capacitated individuals have to make full use of the opportunities. Hence capacitization or capacity building exercise has to be regular at every level in order to cope with the changes that take place in the world. Only by capacitating the people one can think of bridging the gap between and among individuals, groups and societies. Capacity building could be done not only through training but also through activities to energise the people. All activities could be linked with their aspirations or expectations. It is just like profit linked incentives. The incapacitated people's aspirations and expectations will result in deprivation and alienation and the capacitated individuals' aspirations and expectations will end in prosperity.

To achieve prosperity for all in the next millennium, the gap between man and machinery has to be bridged through capacitization process. To share the prosperity with all and to rationalize the utilization of natural resources for prosperity, a micro level institutional mechanism has to be evolved. To channelise the activities of the people, to make use of their energy, and, to achieve prosperity, a pro-nature and a pro-culture framework has to be evolved. Thus the whole exercise is to make man perfect in the evolutionary process. It is a man-making process. To avoid conflicts, assurance to their entitlement of the poor or the deprived or alienated should be ensured through an institutional arrangement which is near to them. Instruments and institutions are to be amenable to the people and their capacity has to be increased to handle them. Every society is grappling with the process of identifying the devices to channelise the energy of the people on a productive basis without any loss to achieve prosperity.

6

CONCLUSION

Society has undergone changes beyond human imagination in the past five decades which have been declared development decades. Human activities have been accelerated to bring about fast changes in society, polity and economy, which will ultimately transform the perception and performance of the people. The transformations are multidimensional in nature and multifaceted in action and they are sustainable in form. These transformations are in the attitude, belief, values and the thought process of the human beings and condition the performance and activities of the people. Of course there are many theories to explain the process of the transformation of the human collectivities. It is natural that academics look at the changes and transformations of the society against the backdrop of the well established theories and frameworks. Yet there are many elements in the process of transformation which are beyond the comprehension of the academics.

More specifically Indian society has its own unique character, which makes the academics nervous while comprehending the transformation of the Indian society as it always provides varieties, variations and unique features which are not patternable. Yet theories have been evolved and developed on the changes the society has witnessed. But the hypotheses deduced from the established theories have not enabled the researchers to concretise the propositions of the theories and they always suffer from ambiguity. As ambivalent ambiguities are many in the existing theories new types of initiatives are made to study the transformations in the Indian society.

While looking at the overall changes in the society and state one notices phenomenal transformation. The phenomenal transformation has puzzled western theorists. The speed of transformation in India in a comparative perspective with other western countries has made the Indians complacent. The macro picture in terms of the achievements of the state and society depict a very green picture on the one hand, and on the other, the hard realities such as struggle against nature, state and society even for basic minimums to lead a human life at the grassroots level indicate a paradox in human progress. Even the basic needs such as food, water, employment, education, right to live and health care are not met for millions of people in this country after fifty years of democratic governance through a variety of schemes and programmes evolved by the bureaucratic elite. This contradiction makes one wonder how far these teeming millions of people participate in the political process or development process.

To understand the reality of the transformation one has to look at the society from the perspective of the perception and performance of the people. Perception and performance of the individuals widely vary in a society like India. Moreover established theories have been questioned through the portrayal of the reality in the Indian society. Poverty has been defined, analysed and explained. Volumes of literature have proliferated. Yet, in India, it has its own significance. People who have been bracketed as the poverty stricken will not have the characteristics of the individuals who are affected by the presence of poverty. People who are rich will not have the characteristics of the rich. They lead a very simple life.

Facilities provided by the government through schemes and programmes have to be utilised fruitfully for the benefit of the poor. The poor have not utilised all the facilities as they do not know the value of the facilities. Schools, roads, medical facilities, cooperatives, banks and communication facilities have been fully utilised by the rich. Hence the poor have not enhanced their capacity to handle the facilities to their advantage.

But, at the same time, by the outward appearance one cannot identify who is poverty stricken and who is not. By the efforts of the government, people started moving from one place to another with or without purpose. The modern facilities provided by the government subtly induce sensory pleasure and people are moving towards achieving the targeted sensory pleasures. In the course of the movement of the people towards modernization and westernization, they have lost sight of the meaningful and harmonious relationship between nature and human beings. The natural order has been totally destroyed and the environment has been degraded. Our scientific and technological advancements have not helped humanity to evolve from one stage to another.

The way in which the society has conducted itself does not demonstrate that the society is moving on a healthy track which will sustain for ever and humanity be perfected continuously. Costumes, cosmetics, literacy, communication, housing facilities, food habits, festivals, and recreations have undergone enormous changes. Well dressed man, educated man, man living in the modern house, using all modern communication facilities, with literacy, has moved into the fray to maximize his profit and to secure maximum facilities for himself.

Government institutions have expanded their size, increased their manpower and enhanced their capacity to manage the human collectivity when they are in interaction to share the benefits of the government. All policies and programmes are oriented towards economic growth and social justice. It is essential to see whether the society has received the basic minimum facilities which are essential for human living. It is to be verified whether the society has achieved livelihood security.

Fifty years have passed after India attained Independence. India has gone on to space research and testing nuclear capacity. Yet, India is not in a position to declare that it has provided the basic facilities such as water, food, education, health and employment to the people. Hence India has two faces, namely the face of America (plenty) and that of Ethiopia (poverty). India is always paradoxical and cannot be easily comprehended.

The changes have been visualised not from the perspective of the academics but against the backdrop of the perception of the people.

This study has brought out the changes in society from the

outlook of the people. There is no valued judgement of the activities of society from the point of view of the researcher. In the western world, material prosperity is the fixed goal and their idea about development is clear and they are pursuing their goal meticulously. But the Indian society has its own inbuilt contradictions in the values and norms of development. They are pursuing economic prosperity as the western society does and, at the same time, highly spiritualised values are deeply rooted in each and every individual. Sometimes it is blended and balanced. Rural poverty is a visualization conceived by the administrators and academics. From the point of view of the people, poverty is nothing but dearth of humanism and lack of understanding, mutual adjustment and toleration.

To achieve what the westerners have achieved, we suggest ways and means and the government chalks out policies and programmes. They are being carried out. The beneficiaries have not perceived the concept of development as conceived by the government. Total confusion gains ground. The government and its organizations have conceived the framework of development as conceived by the westerners. People conceive the framework of development from the ethos of India. Hence moderate speed of transformation, conserving energy, enriching the eco system and achieving sustainable development are the concepts of development perceived by the people. Thus transformation is only an illusion and it could be visualised from any direction and dimension by the outsiders as they like. Human activities in the society would produce results. The results are seen clearly on the material things, and from the material things one would gauge the perception and thought process of the individuals as their ideas are put into practice.

The western materialistic perception has gone deep into the individuals but the moral sentiments of the people, which are innate in the Indian culture, have also gone into the human mind. The interaction between western materialistic perception and Indian moral sentiments is continuously going on in the Indian mind and hence we witness perplexing results in the society in the form of human, socio-economic and political activities. Human collectivities with different age group categories exhibit differing perceptions of what is going on in the society in terms of polity, economy and governance. Pull and pressure work in the society to direct the human collectivity to move from one stage of activities to another. Government institutions are authoritative bodies, which give direction to the prosperity and yet people have not taken all the directives, as their perceptions are dominated by certain values cherished by the community over the years based on their own value system. Thus the society is in a fix between materialistic outlook and moral sentiments. Moral sentiments are the external values which will guide the society.

APPENDICES

APPENDIX-I

FOOD SECURITY AND ENTITLEMENT IN RURAL SOCIETY

Table 1 : Sex of the Respondents

S.No.	Sex	Number	Percentage
1.	Male	159	70.7
2.	Female	66	29.3
	Total	225	100.0

Source : Computed.

Table 2 : Age Group of the Respondents

S.No.	Sex	Number	Percentage
1.	Less than 25	37	16.4
2.	26 - 35	46	20.4
3.	36 - 45	58	25.9
4.	46 - 55	37	16.4
5.	Above 55	47	20.9
	Total	225	100.0

Source : Computed.

Table 3 : Marital Status of the Respondents

S.No.	Status	Number	Percentage
1.	Married	206	91.6
2.	Unmarried	10	4.4
3.	Widow	5	2.2
4.	Widower	2	0.9
5.	Divorce	2	0.9
	Total	225	100.0

Source : Computed.

Table 4 : Community of the Respondents

S.No.	Community	Number	Percentage
1.	Forward Class	Nil	—
2.	Backward Caste	137	60.9
3.	Scheduled Caste	88	39.1
	Total	225	100.0

Source : Computed.

Table 5 : Religion of the Respondents

S.No.	Religion	Number	Percentage
1.	Christian	34	15.1
2.	Hindu	191	84.9
3.	Muslim	Nil	-
	Total	225	100.0

Source : Computed.

Table 6 : Respondents Level of Education

S.No.	Level of Education	Number	Percentage
1.	Illiterate	82	36.4
2.	Primary	54	24.0
3.	Middle	47	20.9
4.	Higher Secondary	29	12.9
5.	Graduates	13	5.8
	Total	225	100.0

Source : Computed.

It is obvious that in most of the occasions entitlements are denied only to the deprived and marginalised as they have no organised support base. Of the 225 respondents near about 50 per cent are agricultural labourers. Their income range is between rupees one and twenty-five thousand. 80 per cent of them belong to this category. As these villages are very near to Gandhigram Rural Institute, the poor use to get facilities from the institute like housing and hence 76 per cent of the respondents have tiled houses. Even after implementing several housing schemes, 15 per cent of them do not have any facility including house.

Table 7 : Respondents and their Occupation

S.No.	Occupation	Number	Percentage
1.	Agriculture	52	23.1
2.	Agricultural Labour	101	44.9
3.	Government Employees	9	4.0
4.	Business	19	8.4
5.	Others	44	19.6
	Total	225	100.0

Source : Computed.

Table 8 : Respondents Income Range

S.No.	Income Range (in Rs.)	Number	Percentage
1.	0 - 25,000	180	80.0
2.	25,001 - 35,000	28	12.4
3.	Above 35,000	17	7.6
	Total	225	100.0

Source : Computed.

Table 9 : Housing Pattern of the Respondents

S.No.	Nature of the House	Number	Percentage
1.	Hut	35	15.5
2.	Tiled	169	76.1
3.	Pucca	19	8.4
4.	Rented	2	0.8
	Total	225	100.8

Source : Computed.

There is a scheme in the government that each and every house is to be electrified in Tamil Nadu. To enable the poor, government have decided that a single light can be provided to the house of the poor at free of cost. It is being implemented in the rural areas. Yet fifty-four houses have not been electrified. It is inferred from the Table 11 that 83 per cent of the respondents are in nuclear family system and 17 per cent are in joint family system. The expansion of family system has created more demands for basic services. Yet another reason that even in the nuclear family the size is not small. It varies from one to five. Yet another aspect one could notice from the Table 13 here is that 47 per cent of the respondents get their food material only through their labour. For their labour they get their food grains.

Table 10 : Electrification of Respondents Houses

S.No.	Electrified House	Number	Percentage
1.	Yes	171	76.0
2.	No	54	24.0
	Total	225	100.0

Source : Computed.

Table 11 : Respondents Family Type

S.No.	Type of Family	Number	Percentage
1.	Nuclear	186	83.0
2.	Joint	39	17.0
	Total	225	100.0

Source : Computed.

Table 12 : Respondents Family Size

S.No.	Family Size	Number	Percentage
1.	1 - 5	189	84.0
2.	6 - 10	36	16.0
	Total	225	100.0

Source : Computed.

Table 13 : Receiving Foodgrains for the Work

S.No.	Food Security	Number	Percentage
1.	Yes	105	47.0
2.	No	120	53.0
	Total	225	100.0

Source : Computed.

Of the 105 respondents, 43 said that availability of food material are inadequate. While asking about the adequacy of purchasing food material near about one-fourth are daily wage earners and they use to purchase food material everyday. For the poor, essential food material are being supplied only through public distribution system and for purchasing the food material one should have ration cards, otherwise their entitlements cannot be ensured. It is interesting to note that near about 32 per cent of the respondents have no ration cards and they said that same number of cards are available with influential persons in the same villages. It is a pity that there is no mechanism to check and render justice to the poor by way of providing ration cards.

Table 14 : Adequacy of Foodgrains

S.No.	Adequacy	Number	Percentage
1.	Yes	62	28.0
2.	No	43	19.0
	Total	105	47.0

Source : Computed.

Table 15 : Frequency of Purchase

S.No.	Frequency	Number	Percentage
1.	Purchasing daily	159	26.0
2.	Weekly	166	74.0
	Total	225	100.0

Source : Computed.

Table 16 : Managing the Additional Expenditure

S.No.	Means	Number	Percentage
1.	Through loans	109	48.0
2.	Adjustment	731	9.0
3.	Mortgaging articles	433	3.0
	Total	225	100.0

Source : Computed.

Table 17 : Possession of Ration Cards

S.No.	Possession	Number	Percentage
1.	Yes	152	68.0
2.	No	73	32.0
	Total	225	100.0

Source : Computed.

Of the total respondents 36 per cent of them informed that they find it difficult to get needed food material. Even though they have facilities and space to store food grains, they could not find resources to purchase food grains and store them at their disposal. While considering the stocking period, one can easily make an observation that the people have the capacity to purchase food material only for a period of four weeks. Their saving capacity is poor as majority of them are farm labourers. Moreover they use to store only rice and not other items of food materials.

Table 18 : Getting Food Materials Regularly

S.No.	Getting their dues	Number	Percentage
1.	Yes	145	64.0
2.	No	80	36.0
	Total	225	100.0

Source : Computed.

Table 19 : Facilities to store Foodgrains

S.No.	Storing Facility	Number	Percentage
1.	Yes	179	29.0
2.	No	46	21.0
	Total	225	100.0

Source : Computed.

Table 20 : Availability of Foodgrains

S.No.	Availability	Number	Percentage
1.	Yes	120	67.0
2.	No	59	33.0
	Total	179	100.0

Source : Computed.

Table 21 : Stocking Period

S.No.	Stocking Period	Number	Percentage
1.	One week	46	38.0
2.	1 - 2 weeks	17	14.0
3.	2 - 3 weeks	8	8.0
4.	3 - 4 weeks	17	14.0
5.	More than 4 weeks	31	26.0
	Total	120	100.0

Source : Computed.

Table 22 : Foodgrains Stored

S.No.	Foodgrains	Number	Percentage
1.	Paddy	20	10.0
2.	Sorghum	23	10.0
3.	Ragi	4	2.0
4.	Millets	12	5.0
5.	Rice	166	73.0
	Total	225	100.0

Source : Computed.

Table 23 : Frequency of Taking Food

S.No.	Frequency	Number	Percentage
1.	One time a day	2	0.8
2.	Two times a day	94	41.7
3.	Three times a day	129	57.3
	Total	225	99.8

Source : Computed.

Of the respondents, 41 per cent of them are having the habit of taking food only two times a day as they have the capacity to meet such expenditure only. Now they are habituated to take food only two times a day. It is curious to note that even though they take food two times and three times a day, while analysing the content of the food it is inferred that the food items consumed by the people are not having nutritive value.

Table 24 : Consuming Nutritious Food

S.No.	Category	Number	Percentage
1.	Yes	57	25.0
2.	No	168	75.0
	Total	225	100.0

Source : Computed.

Table 25 : Adequacy of Quality Food

S.No.	Adequacy	Number	Percentage
1.	Yes	33	15.0
2.	No	24	10.0
	Total	57	25.0

Source : Computed.

Table 26 : Respondents' Ownership Status of Housing

S.No.	Housing	Number	Percentage
1.	Own	195	87.0
2.	Rented	3	1.0
3.	Government allotted	27	12.0
	Total	225	100.0

Source : Computed.

Table 27 : Details of Patta Received by Respondents

S.No.	Nature of Patta	Number	Percentage
1.	Yes	133	59.0
2.	No	54	24.0
3.	Own house	38	17.0
	Total	225	100.0

Source : Computed.

Government has many schemes to provide financial assistance to the poor. Of the respondents 92 per cent of them said that majority of them have not availed the government loan facilities and only a handful of people have been repeatedly receiving the benefits continuously.

Table 28 : Financial Assistance Availed

S.No.	Financial Assistance	Number	Percentage
1.	Yes	18	8.0
2.	No	207	92.0
	Total	225	100.0

Source : Computed.

Water is basic and fundamental commodity which is an entitlement of the people. Even after fifty years of our democratic governance the government is not in a position to make an announcement that it has provided water for all. But in Tamil Nadu conditions are different. All are getting water for their use.

Table 29 : Sources of Drinking Water

S.No.	Source of Drinking Water	Number	Percentage
1.	Hand pump + Tank	180	80.0
2.	Local well	19	8.0
3.	Private well	16	7.0
4.	Private tap	10	5.0
	Total	225	100.0

Source : Computed.

But the problem is, whether we are providing safe and protected drinking water? For this question one cannot get positive reply from the people. 47 per cent of the people are not getting the needed and protected water supply. 68 per cent of the respondents said that they are not able to get adequate water supply. The respondents do not know how to test the water also and hence in most of the occasions they are not aware of the quality of water they consume. In the same way 80 per cent of the respondents felt that they are not aware of how to maintain the overhead tank and how to clean it and how often water is to be chlorinated.

Table 30 : Status of Water Quality

S.No.	Water Quality	Number	Percentage
1.	Soft	120	53.0
2.	Hard	105	47.0
	Total	225	100.0

Source : Computed.

Table 31 : Availability of Water

S.No.	Availability	Number	Percentage
1.	Adequate	71	32.0
2.	Inadequate	154	68.0
	Total	225	100.0

Source : Computed.

Table 32 : Knowledge of Respondents with regard to Water Test

S.No.	Knowledge	Number	Percentage
1.	Yes	16	7.0
2.	No	182	80.0
3.	Don't know	27	13.0
	Total	225	100.0

Source : Computed.

Table 33 : Details of Chlorination

S.No.	Chlorination	Number	Percentage
1.	Yes	45	20.0
2.	No	123	55.0
3.	Don't know	57	25.0
	Total	225	100.0

Source : Computed.

Generally one would feel that a pucca drainage is essential for urban areas and not for rural areas as the soil has got the capacity to absorb the drained water. When natural flow was not disturbed, the drainage water will lead to its destination and it will move out from the village. But now the human settlement obstructed the natural arrangement and hence water flow is arrested and as a result everywhere water is stagnated. The stagnated water produces flies. No proper attention was given for drainage. 69 per cent of the respondents said that there is no drainage system for their habitat.

Toilet is, yet another interesting observation. Toilets are basic and essential facilities and yet the importance was not known to the people. Moreover, the governments were also not in a position to realise its importance. Now it gains momentum. 90 per cent of the respondents said that there is no toilet facility either in their houses individually or collectively for the community. As a result the villages are spoiled by their open air defocation.

Noon meal scheme for the students is a service programme and this programme has not reached to all the needy persons.

Table 34 : Availability of Drainage

S.No.	Availability	Number	Percentage
1.	Yes	69	31.0
2.	No	156	69.0
	Total	225	100.0

Source : Computed.

Table 35 : Availability of Toilet Facilities

S.No.	Availability	Number	Percentage
1.	Yes	23	10.0
2.	No	202	90.0
	Total	225	100.0

Source : Computed.

Table 36 : Respondents Children availing Noon-meal Scheme

S.No.	Availed or not	Number	Percentage
1.	Yes	149	66.0
2.	No	76	34.0
	Total	225	100.0

Source : Computed.

Table 37 : Livelihood Status of Landless

S.No.	Adequate Livelihood	Number	Percentage
1.	Yes	19	8.0
2.	No	206	92.0
	Total	225	100.0

Source : Computed.

The landless labourers in the rural areas have to migrate many times in a year to distant places for want of employment opportunities. Only 9 per cent of the respondents said that they are able to find employment opportunity locally. The migration has created number of problems in their family and more particularly it affects the studies of their children.

India is in the higher order in textile industry but it does not mean that all individuals in the society is ensured with adequate clothing. 43 per cent of them said that in the villages there are people with inadequate cloth. Medical care is the responsibility of the state. Hence government shows keen interest in creating health facilities. Yet these facilities are not reaching the people. If the people have money they will manage on their own but they do not have adequate money for health care.

Human beings are wearing chapals for their foots with a purpose of protecting them. But in India it is a status symbol. People started wearing chapal in the recent years irrespective of their social status. 33 per cent of the respondents said that they are not wearing chapals.

Table 38 : Landless Labour Families Going out for Employment

S.No.	Going out for Employment	Number	Percentage
1.	50 - 100	197	88.0
2.	101 - 150	8	3.0
3.	Local Employment	20	9.0
	Total	225	100.0

Source : Computed.

Table 39 : Adequacy of Cloth

S.No.	Adequacy	Number	Percentage
1.	Yes	128	57.0
2.	No	97	43.0
	Total	225	100.0

Source : Computed.

Table 40 : Adequacy of Money for Medical Care

S.No.	Adequacy	Number	Percentage
1.	Yes	35	16.0
2.	No	190	84.0
	Total	225	100.0

Source : Computed.

Table 41 : Wearing of Chapal

S.No.	Respondents opinion	Number	Percentage
1.	Yes	151	67.0
2.	No	74	33.0
	Total	225	100.0

Source : Computed.

Table 42 : Condition of the Link Road

S.No.	Condition	Number	Percentage
1.	BT	107	48.0
2.	Metal	42	19.0
3.	Earth	76	33.0
	Total	225	100.0

Source : Computed.

Table 43 : Encroachment on Footpath/Cart-road

S.No.	Encroachment	Number	Percentage
1.	Yes	68	30.0
2.	No	157	70.0
	Total	225	100.0

Source : Computed.

Table 44 : Availability of Waiting Shed for Passengers

S.No.	Availability	Number	Percentage
1.	Yes	153	68.0
2.	No	72	32.0
	Total	225	100.0

Source : Computed.

In Tamil Nadu the availability of transport even in the nook and corner is adequate as per the popular perception but in reality it is not so. 51 per cent of the respondents said that they have to walk a few miles to take a bus even though road facilities are available. It is interesting to note that there are adequate number of waiting sheds for the passengers who travel in buses in Tamil Nadu.

Table 45 : Availability of Bus Service

S.No.	Availability	Number	Percentage
1.	Yes	110	49.0
2.	No	115	51.0
	Total	225	100.0

Source : Computed.

Table 46 : Frequency of Bus Service

S.No.	Adequate	Number	Percentage
1.	Yes	59	26.0
2.	No	51	23.0
	Total	110	49.0

Source : Computed.

Table 47 : Number of Respondents Made Complaint to Authority

S.No.	Complained or not	Number	Percentage
1.	Yes	82	36.0
2.	No	33	15.0
	Total	115	51.0

Source : Computed.

Post office and telecommunication are two important public facilities to communicate messages from one place to another. 85 per cent of the respondents said that they do not have post office in their nearby village and likewise 80 per cent of them said that they have no telephone facility.

Table 48 : Availability of Post Office

S.No.	Availability	Number	Percentage
1.	Yes	35	15.0
2.	No	190	85.0
	Total	225	100.0

Source : Computed.

Table 49 : Availability of Telephone Booth

S.No.	Availability	Number	Percentage
1.	Yes	45	20.0
2.	No	180	80.0
	Total	225	100.0

Source : Computed.

Table 50 : Opinion on Old Age Pension

S.No.	Needed/Not needed	Number	Percentage
1.	Yes	157	70.0
2.	No	68	30.0
	Total	225	100.0

Source : Computed.

Table 51 : Status of Street Light Facilities

S.No.	Status	Number	Percentage
1.	Adequate	7	3.0
2.	Inadequate	218	97.0
	Total	225	100.0

Source : Computed.

Table 52 : Number of Respondents who made Complaint

S.No.	Details	Number	Percentage
1.	Complained	84	38.0
2.	Not complained	103	47.0
3.	Panchayat President	31	15.0
	Total	225	100.0

Source : Computed.

Like shelter, water and streets, streetlights are so important for the people for their mobility during the nights. 97 per cent of the respondents said that there is no adequate street lights in their area. They further informed that even the available street lights are not in good condition.

Table 53 : Condition of Street Lights

S.No.	Condition	Number	Percentage
1.	Good	8	3.0
2.	Bad	217	97.0
	Total	225	100.0

Source : Computed.

Gender equality is ensured as per the provisions of the Constitution. But in reality it is not ensured. 63 per cent of the respondents said that women are not treated equally on par with men.

Table 54 : Perception on Women Equality in the Society

S.No.	Respondents opinion	Number	Percentage
1.	Yes	81	37.0
2.	No	144	63.0
	Total	225	100.0

Source : Computed.

Table 55 : Consult Women in the Families

S.No.	Respondents Opinion	Number	Percentage
1.	Yes	137	61.0
2.	No	88	39.0
	Total	225	100.0

Source : Computed.

Table 56 : Perception on SC/ST

S.No.	Respondents Opinion	Number	Percentage
1.	Yes	105	47.0
2.	No	120	53.0
	Total	225	100.0

Source : Computed.

Common properties are lifeline of the poor and the marginalised. It is the responsibility of the state to make the common properties accessible to the poor. 52 per cent of the respondents said that the common properties are not very nearer to the marginalised and deprived.

Table 57 : Accessibility of Common Properties to SC/ST

S.No.	Respondents Opinion	Number	Percentage
1.	Yes	109	48.0
2.	No	116	52.0
	Total	225	100.0

Source : Computed.

Yet another aspect is social recognition is being found. In the villages the SC and ST community cannot enter into the temples. Still they are not permitted to enter into the temples. Hence separate temples have been constructed for the SC and ST.

Table 58 : Accessibility of Village Temples to all SC/ST

S.No.	Respondents Opinion	Number	Percentage
1.	Yes	12	5.0
2.	No	126	39.0
3.	Separate	87	56.0
	Total	225	100.0

Source : Computed.

Table 59 : Respondents Possessing Milch Animals

S.No.	Possession	Number	Percentage
1.	Yes	168	75.0
2.	No	57	25.0
	Total	225	100.0

Source : Computed.

Table 60 : Availability of Animal Husbandry Hospital

S.No.	Availability	Number	Percentage
1.	Yes	35	15.0
2.	No	190	85.0
	Total	225	100.0

Source : Computed.

Table 61 : Conditions of Graveyard

S.No.	Condition	Number	Percentage
1.	Good	19	8.0
2.	Bad	206	92.0
	Total	225	100.0

Source : Computed.

Table 62 : Availability of Approach Road

S.No.	Availability	Number	Percentage
1.	Yes	55	24.0
2.	No	170	76.0
	Total	225	100.0

Source : Computed.

Table 63 : Membership in Cooperative Agriculture Society

S.No.	Membership	Number	Percentage
1.	Yes	23	10.0
2.	No	202	90.0
	Total	225	100.0

Source : Computed.

Table 64 : Utilizing the Services of the Societies

S.No.	Respondents Opinion	Number	Percentage
1.	Yes	18	8.0
2.	No	207	92.0
	Total	225	100.0

Source : Computed.

Table 65 : Number of Land holders among the Respondents

S.No.	Landholders	Number	Percentage
1.	Yes	63	28.0
2.	No	162	72.0
	Total	225	100.0

Source : Computed.

Table 66 : Extension of Land Owned by the Respondents

S.No.	Land in acres	Wet land	Dry land
1.	1/2	18	14.0
2.	1	8	5.0
3.	2	8	6.0
4.	More than 2	6	8.0
	Total	30	33.0

Source : Computed.

Table 67 : Opinion on the Representation of Poor Men in Local Units of Political Parties

S.No.	Respondents Opinion	Number	Percentage
1.	Yes	97	43.0
2.	No	128	57.0
	Total	225	100.0

Source : Computed.

APPENDIX - II

A. VILLAGE PROFILE - NARIUTHU

1. General Particulars

Village Name	:	Nariuthu
Panchayat	:	Nariuthu
Block	:	Nilakottai
District	:	Dindigul

2. Total No. of families

Total	:	200
BC	:	75
SC	:	125

3. Caste Distribution of families : Goundar/Pillaimar/Chettiar/Pallar/Sakkiliyar

4. Structure of the house: Hut/Kutcha/mixed (Only 30 houses electrified)

5. Population Details

Male	:	250
Female	:	150
Total	:	400

6. Irrigation sources

Well	:	3
Hand pump	:	3

7. Educational Institutions : Management school - 1 (elementary level)

8. Communication facilities
   Branch post office : 1
   T.V. Room : 2 (SC - 1 and BC - 1)

9. Tea stall : 2

10. Temple : 3 Famous temples (Muthalamman Festival)

B. VILLAGE PROFILE OF BALAMPATTI

1. General Particulars
   Village Name : Balampatti
   Panchayat : Nariuthu
   Block : Nilakottai

2. Total No. of families : 150
   BC : 100
   SC : 50

3. Caste distribution : Goundar/Chettiar/Asari/Nadar/Vannan/Barbar/Sakkiliyar/Pandaram

4. Structure of the house: Hut/kutcha/mixed

5. Population details
   Total : 650
   Male : 375
   Female : 275

6. Soil condition : Red soil
   Wet land : Avarai, Flower
   Dry land : Sorghum, Kambu

7. Irrigation sources

Well	:	5
Hand pump	:	4
Pond	:	2

8. Educational institutions

Management elementary school	:	1
ICDS Centre	:	1

9. Marketing Facilities

Tea stall	:	4
Grocery shop	:	3
Fertilizer shop	:	1

10. Village Organization

Youth club	:	1
Mahalir Mandram	:	1

C. VILLAGE PROFILE OF KATTUNAICKANPATTI

1.	Village Name	:	Kattunaickanpatti
	Panchayat	:	Nariuthu
	Block	:	Nilakottai
2.	Total No. of families	:	109
	Christian	:	16
	Hindu	:	93
3.	Caste distribution	:	Vaduga Naidu/Thottia Naicker
4.	Structure of the house	:	Hut/kutcha mixed
5.	Population details		
	Male	:	258
	Female	:	245
	Total	:	503

6.	Soil type	:	Red soil
	Major Crops	:	
	Wet land'	:	Grapes, Avarai
	Dry land	:	Sorgam, Kambu, gingelly, guava
7.	Major source of irrigation		
	Well	:	2
	Hand pump	:	3
8.	Educational institution		
	Panchayat Union School	:	1
	Gandhigram Trust Balwadi Centre	:	1
9.	Marketing facilities		
	Tea stall	:	1
10.	Village Organizations	:	
	Voluntary organisation	:	1

D. VILLAGE PROFILE OF UCHANAMPATTI

1.	Village Name	:	Uchanampatti
	Panchayat	:	Nariuthu
	Block	:	Nilakottai
2.	No. of families	:	270
	BC	:	153
	SC	:	117
3.	Caste distribution	:	Goundar/Chettiar/Asari/Thevar/ Nadar/SC-Pallar/Parayar
4.	Structure of the house	:	Hut/kutcha mixed (70% of the houses are electrified)

5. Population details

Male	:	612
Female	:	628
Total	:	1240

6. Irrigation facilities

Well	:	1
Hand pump	:	4

7. Educational Institutions

Union Elementary School	:	1
ICDS Centre	:	1

8. Marketing facilities

Tea stall	:	2
Grocery shop	:	3

9. Dairy farm : 1

10. Temple : 4

11. Village organization

Mahalir mandram	:	1

BIBLIOGRAPHY

Baden-Powell, B.H. 1896, *The Indian Village Community,* London: Longmans.

Beteille, A. 1965, *Caste, Class and Power : Changing Patterns of Stratification in a Tanjure Village,* Berkeley : University of California Press.

Breman, J. *et al.* eds. 1997, *The Village in Asia Revisited,* New Delhi : Oxford University Press.

Dube, S. C. 1955, *Indian Village,* London : Routledge and Kegan Paul.

Dube, S. C., 1988, *Modernization and Development : The Search for Alternative Paradigms,* New Delhi : Vistaar Publications.

Dube, S. C. 1958, *India's Changing Villages : Human Factors in Community Development,* London : Routledge and Kegan Paul.

Epstein T. Scarlett, Surya Narayana, A. P., Timmegowda, T. 1998, *Village Voices : Forty Years of Rural Transformation in South India,* New Delhi : Sage Publications.

Fuller, C. J. 1989, *Caste Today,* New Delhi : Oxford University Press.

Marriott, M. ed. 1955, *Village India : Studies in the Little Community,* Chicago : Chicago University Press.

Moore, E. 1985, *Conflict and Compromise Justice in an Indian Village,* Berkeley : University of California Press.

Madan, Vandana, ed., 2002, *The Village India,* New Delhi : Oxford University Press.

Srinivas, M. N. 1998, *Village, Caste, Gender and Method,* New Delhi : Oxford University Press.

Srinivas, M. N. 1966, *Social Change in Modern India,* Berkeley : University of California Press.

Srinivas, M. N. 1960, *Indian Villages,* Bombay : Asia Publishing House.

Slater, G. 1921, *Some South Indian Villages,* Madras : Madras University Publications.

Yugandhar, B. N. and Neela Mukherjee eds. 1991, *Studies in Village India,* New Delhi : Concept Publishing Company.

Wade, R. 1988, *Village Republics,* Cambridge : Cambridge University Press.

INDEX